HEAVEN IS REAL

Introduction.........
Chapter One ....Learn How Heaven Helps Us
Chapter Two ....Aspects of the Soul
Chapter Three .....Premonitions
Chapter Four ......Climate Change and COVID-19
Chapter Five.......Angels at Work
Chapter Six ....Sensing Angels
Chapter Seven .... Life Plan Analysis
Chapter Eight......The Miracle of Clairvoyance
Chapter Nine.......Discovering the Meaning of Life
Chapter Ten ...... First Heaven
Chapter Eleven ..Life Plan Readings
Chapter Twelve ... Past Lives
Chapter Thirteen..The Clairvoyant
Chapter Fourteen ..Hauntings
Chapter Fifteen....The Big Questions, the Bigger Picture
Chapter Sixteen... Heaven is Real
Chapter Seventeen... Clairvoyant Poetry

Copyright Robert Mason 2021

INTRODUCTION

This book is an account of how I discovered, through over forty years of research, the meaning of life and the reality of Heaven. My research has led me to believe beyond doubt that we all have a spiritual consciousness and that there is an Afterlife that can be described as "Heaven". Heaven is real.

This acccount is intended for those who do not hold strong religious beliefs, and are open minded to the most reassuring and wonderful truths revealed in this book. The research discoveries are a good and positive study that concentrates on understanding what is really going on in our lives that has a purpose that originates in our true home, the spiritual Afterlife of Heaven. For those who are apprehensive concerning spiritual matters, please be reassured that throughout this book are insights that are totally safe to study because they have been given to me from messages sent in unconditional love by those who are in Heaven.
We live in a world where many people no longer hold religious beliefs. The basic questions such as "Do we have a soul?" "Is there an Afterlife?". "Does God exist?", and "Is there a Heaven?" are questions that most people prefer not to think about. Perhaps it is easier just to get on with living rather than contemplate spiritual matters.

Religions teach their beliefs, yet different faiths often disagree with each other.

When I was younger, I started a quest of spiritual research to discover the answers to these questions. I thought that the Christian Church would give me the answers, so I became actively involved with several Churches, eventually training to be a Methodist Preacher.

I am no longer involved with the Churches, but my faith had taught me that entry to Heaven is conditional on many things, including being a good Christian and attending Church regularly. I would speak with Christian colleagues' concerning what might happen to the souls of non-Christians. The uncomfortable conclusion was that those souls would not be able to enter Heaven and would therefore cease to exist.

As a part of my research, I studied every piece of information I could concerning human spiritual experiences. I read several books describing cases where people had experienced "Near Death Experiences (NDE)". There are many people who have had an NDE and are reluctant to talk about it for fear of ridicule. I spoke personally with several people who had been through an NDE, and I found that they were typically experienced by people who had been close to death through illness or accident and had been saved by modern medical help. Their experiences were reported as being life changing, and the descriptions of where their soul travelled were of a Heaven-like place. Furthermore, the descriptions of Heaven were remarkably similar in almost every case. Most accounts were from people who did not have a strong religious faith. I questioned: "How is it possible that people with no religious faith can experience Heaven? After all, the teachings of many of the Churches is that reaching Heaven is conditional, and that even some Christians don't do enough to be granted a place in Heaven.

My spiritual research recognised that science could never find proof of Heaven because Heaven is in another dimension. Instead, I would reach logical conclusions based on observing and recording human spiritual experiences.

The Vision

I was totally unprepared for what happened to me on 1st May 1999 when I experienced a vision that changed my life forever. I felt myself, my soul being lifted into the Heavens. I was shown that there is more than one Heaven. I was given the answer to my questions concerning survival of the soul, and of Heaven. I describe this vision fully later in the book. What came from the vision is that there is more than one Heaven.

The Higher Heavens

In my vision I was shown the Higher Heavens. Holy Scripture says that Jesus rose up to the Third Heaven. I was told that souls who had led a perfect life would ascend to the Higher Heavens when they pass away from their life as a human being. Religious faiths might teach people that this "True Heaven" is what we should hope for. The vision was clear that souls must be genuinely good and caring in their love for others, for nature, and for our beautiful Earth in order to reach the Higher Heavens, irrespective of their beliefs. People might ask "What is Higher Heaven Like?". I can only reply that it is what might be described by their religious faith.

First Heaven

The most amazing part of the vision was to be shown and described to me as "First Heaven". This is a very beautiful place and appears like Earth with a landscape of flowers, trees, valleys and all of nature radianting life energies as if on a Spring morning.

Unconditional love is a very real energy that we can feel. Most souls reach this place at the end of their life as a human being irrespective of whether they held a religious faith. Souls can rest in this place to recover from life and rebuild their energies. Souls can also look over loved-ones who are still alive in their human life. Our Guardian Angels who accompany us throughout life can be seen in First Heaven. We realise that First Heaven is our familar home where we came from before birth and now return. We were given life for the experience, for adventure, and to learn so many things. Our soul must reincarnate eventualy to live another life as a human being in order to continue our learning and our true spiritual development.

I go on to describe First Heaven during the remainder of this book. I can see through to First Heaven, and I see the Angels, whereas I can only get a glimpse of the Higher Heavens.

At the time of my vision I received the gift of clairvoyant ability, when previously I was very sceptical of clairvoyants. This has been an experience that has felt like a miracle and has given me the ability to see Angels and bring people messages from the Angels that are similar to clairvoyant readings. It has also given me the ability to work with our Guardian Angels to be shown some of the future, and receive premonitions. I have gained a huge amount of knowledge about who and what we are, and about the Spiritual Realm of Heaven. This has helped me understand what I see when the Guardian Angels are helping me.

TUNING IN TO HEAVEN

As I previously explained this book is not about religion. I am a spiritual researcher and I constantly look for logical explanations before I come to tentative conclusions. My very real spiritual experiences that subsequently came from my Vision have given me personal proof of the Heavens.

Many people use the term "Afterlife" as a general description for a life that our soul will move on to after our physical life ends.
The term "Afterlife" embraces all possible spiritual experiences after we leave our physical life. In my research I have discovered that most souls reach First Heaven, even though their lives may have been far from perfect. Perhaps one person in ten thousand might choose not to go directly to Heaven because of some traumatic end to their life or because of evil deeds that they committed in life. Negative, evil energy does exist on the earth plane in pockets, whereas Heaven is infinite.
Throughout the remainder of this book I will refer to First Heaven as "Heaven".
Heaven is another dimension where love is felt as a real, natural energy. It is our familiar true home where we came from before birth. Heaven is a separate place, but it also all around us. We are surrounded in life by spiritual energies that most people are quite blind to. Some of the energies are negative, evil energies which is why we should never open ourselves up to evil. Often, when a person does bad things such as hurting others, they find it easy to feed off negative energies that seem to boost their ability to continue doing bad things.
I will explain how we can learn to discern between negative energies and the energies of Heaven. By tuning into the energies of Heaven we can access the most powerful help.
This book explains how we can tune in to Heaven, the benefits of which are life changing. We may lose the fear of our mortality. We may begin to access true spiritual guidance and help from Heaven. Those in Heaven whom we may call "Guardian Angels" are accompanied by other loving spiritual beings who simply try to help us through life. They communicate through our feelings, our intuition and our conscience. They try to bring healing to us. They can also help us see the future in some significant ways, and importantly, guide us to change our futures for the better.
Learning to "Tune-in" to Heaven is described throughout this book. With an open mind, determination and love for others and nature you may discover a gradual move forward in life to-

it would be VV Good

HEAVEN IS REAL

wards Heaven-sent spiritual empowerment beyond your wildest dreams!

During the early years of my research, I made an amateur study of Quantum Physics, and was fascinated by the theories of parallel universes, and observations that the tiniest particles of matter appeared to behave in strange ways. At sub-atomic level the tiniest particles of matter can appear from nowhere and disappear into seemingly nowhere.
I began to visualise solid objects around me in a different way. Everything is made of unimaginable vast amounts of energy within the atoms. Invisible energy that holds things together. I could look at a wooden table, and then visualise it as semi-transparent with nothing in between the atoms and molecules except invisible energy.
I thought about radio and television signals travelling through the air at the speed of light, carrying vast amount of information, yet we see and feel nothing unless we have equipment that can convert these signals back into video and audio.
I read that Quantum Mechanics has a theory that is named "The Spooky Theory". An electron can cause another electron at the other side of the universe to instantly move in the same way at the same time. We make use of the Spooky Theory when using any electrical device such as a phone, when using apps, and when using any computer. Have you ever questioned how messaging, or use of apps is an instantaneous process? Most people just accept these things without asking questions.

All these observations show us that our physical senses are quite limited. Our eyes pick-up light, our ears pick-up sound. Then we have the senses of smell, taste and touch, and that's it!
I began to realise that we can't see, hear, touch, smell or taste spiritual energies that are very real.

Who or what are we?
Our soul energy is made of the same stuff that I call "Conscious

Energy" that populates the Spiritual Realm of Heaven. This is nothing spooky or weird, and nothing to be frightened about because Heaven is our true home.

An important gift when learning about Heaven is the gift of Discernment between good spiritual energies, and negative, evil spiritual energies. Negative energies are not allowed into Heaven. Sometimes evil can often show itself as good so the ability to truly discern is an acquired skill that must be gradually developed.

There are spiritual energies around us all the time, mainly from the Angels, helping, guiding and constantly trying to heal and sustain life, including ourselves.
Life energies are programmed – like a computer operating system. Our body is the "Hardware", and our everyday tasks are the "Application Software" or "Apps". Unseen Life Energies keep our body working and bring-in healing from the Angels.

In our everyday experience as human beings we may not notice the faint spiritual energies at the outer edge of our perception.
With enhanced knowledge of Heaven, and the Angels we can look out for these energies and learn the first steps in recognising them.
There is an almost impenetrable barrier between the dimension of Heaven, and the physical universe in which we are temporarily in life dwelling. I say "Almost" because there are energies there that we can, with the correct knowledge, recognise, interpret, and respond to.
Much of the spiritual activity that can be sensed is from the Angels, especially our own Guardian Angels.

Are We Spiritual?

The most basic questions are all connected: Are we spiritual? Is there a Heaven? Is there any form of spiritual afterlife?

Science tells us that we do not have a soul and that a spiritual realm cannot exist because physical science is unable to find evidence that these exist. The most common ways that human beings can accept that there is a spiritual dimension and that we ourselves have a soul are through either religious beliefs or personal spiritual experiences. In modern times so called "Near Death Experiences" have become widely recorded. This is because many people who have been near death due to injury or serious illness have been saved by modern day professional medical help. During their time at the closest point to death some estimates indicate that around 17% of people experience an out-of-body spiritual event that can be recalled later. These NDE experiences can be totally convincing and life changing. Sometimes those experiencing an NDE can recall seeing their Guardian Angel.

The following is an account of a NDE based on a true experience: Peter was proud of his motor bike and travelled everywhere on it, including travel to work. Kate, his girlfriend constantly worried about him riding his bike because he seemed oblivious to danger, especially in bad weather situations. The day that he had his accident was a weekend and he decided to visit his parents who lived 9 miles away from his home. The weather was quite bad with heavy rain and strong winds as he travelled on a country road out of town. His bike suddenly hit a bump in the road that knocked his steering. The bike started to swerve uncontrollably on the wet road surface. He came off the road and hit a tree and everything went black.

Peter found himself awake in hospital. He was looking down at a hospital bed with a doctor and two nurses attending someone who was unconscious. It took he a moment to realise that the person they were attending was himself. He didn't feel concerned, nor did he feel afraid. He felt good and yet he knew what the doctor and nurses were thinking. The nurses were thinking "He won't make it. He is going to die". The doctor was thinking "I will try my best to save him".

Peter found himself being drawn to a light at the side of the room. The light seemed warm and inviting as he entered its loving embrace. He was moving at high speed in what seemed like a tunnel at the end of which was the source of the light. He could see the vague outline of two people stood in the light. Suddenly he found himself in a calm, beautiful meadow. His soul had entered the gateway to Heaven. The grass was green, and flowers of every shade seemed to shine with a vivid intensity that left him lost for words. Peter was surprised at how he felt. All his senses were working yet he had no physical body. His soul energy was his body. He felt as though this was the true reality of home. Unconditional love was around him like the air that he had breathed in life. Peter also experienced a profound feeling of oneness with the universe.

He was met by his grandma who he knew had died last year. His grandad was stood with her. He had died nine years earlier. "It is not your time" said his grandma. Peter felt totally unconcerned about the life he had just left. "Can I stay here" said Peter. His grandma did not reply as a spiritual being appeared in the form of person but radiating light and he felt that this was an Angel. The Angel had no wings and appeared as a man with white and purple radiant garments and a presence that felt loving but strict, with some spiritual authority. "You have things to do that we planned for you in your life. You must go back" said the Angel. "Are you my Guardian Angel?" asked Peter. Before he received a response, he suddenly felt himself much heavier and began to feel some discomfort and pain. He opened his eyes and realised that he was back in his body in a hospital bed. A nurse saw that he had regained consciousness and he heard her say to a colleague "He is awake, thank goodness, I thought we had lost him".

Peter eventually made a full recovery although he never rode a motor bike again. He was reluctant to tell people about his NDE, but he did tell his girlfriend Kate. Kate was the person who told me about this when she came to me for an Angel messages reading. During the reading I was given a message that her boyfriend had been injured in a motor incident and that it had changed his life. She confirmed to me that Peter had experienced this life changing event and that it had made him more caring towards her and others. Peter was no longer scared at the thought of death, but now knew that it was only the beginning of another stage in the eternal life of his true inner being.

The following is a further true account of an NDE, but a different experience:

Alison was on holiday with her sister at a popular seaside holiday resort on the south coast of England. The weather was hot and sunny, so they headed for the beach. There were lifeguard stations so the two felt totally at ease as they walked into the sea. "I'll race you swimming up to that buoy" said her sister Carol. The buoy floated bright orange about two hundred yards off the beach. It was probably something securing a fishing pot for catching lobsters or crabs. Alison reached the buoy first and turned to see Carol approaching her and looking frustrated because she came second. The girls, both aged in their twenties, held position together at the buoy. "The water is cold" shouted Alison. "Come on let's get back to the beach and warm up in the sun". "You go first" she said to Carol. "I will still try to win".

Carol lunged forward to swim towards the beach in the cold sea water. Alison waited a few seconds then struck forward to swim back. Suddenly her arms and legs went into severe cramp. The shock of the cold sea was hitting her. She struggled to keep swimming but the harder she tried the more her arms and legs screamed with pain. She could no longer swim and found herself being submerged. She tried to get her head above water and screamed for help. The cold sea started to swallow her. It seemed quite deep and small waves that she hadn't really noticed were hindering her attempts to gasp a mouthful of air. She realised she was drowning and going under. Her senses of panic overwhelmed her. In her mind her life flashed before her. Every minute of her life could be vividly seen, ending in her sadness at the memory of her daughter, now aged two years, at home with her partner Mike who was at home while she took a day out with her sister.

The pain in her limbs disappeared and then she felt herself in a place of blackness. She couldn't understand what has happened to her but didn't feel frightened. A small light appeared in the distance, racing towards her and getting bigger as it approached. The light quickly reached her, and she felt at ease and surrounded by light. The light enveloped like a warm blanket of love as she saw in the light her father who had died the previous year. "It's not your time Alison. Tell your mother I love her and that I still watch over her". A beautiful spiritual being then came into view. Without words she knew it was her Guardian Angel who knew everything about her, her good and bad, and loved her unconditionally for whom she was and is.

The moment in the gateway to Heaven came to and ended as she awoke coughing up sea water, gasping for breath. She felt cold like she had never been before, and her breathing was painful. She was alive. The lifeguards had been quick to act when they heard her screams before she went under the water. Carol was with her and held her hand as she was taken by stretcher into an ambulance and then on to the local A&E hospital.

After an overnight stay in hospital Alison made a full recovery.

Many months later she came to see me for a reading. Her father came through and her Guardian Angel brought through a vision of this incident that Alison confirmed as correct. Her life had been changed forever by her near-death experience and she felt spiritually stronger. Alison was happy and deeply moved emotionally to hear messages from her father.

As with most people who have experienced an NDE she now seemed to value every moment of every day as a blessing and life as a precious gift. Her experience of life flashing before her eyes as she was drowning has led to questions in my spiritual research. This is quite a common experience.

Question to Heaven: "Why do some people see their life flashing before them at the time of near death?

Message from Heaven: "The human brain has a memory and so does the spiritual soul of a person. At the time of near death, the brain is programmed to upload as much memory as possible to the soul. The memory bank of life experiences is important to the soul as the person transitions back from physical life to Heaven. The brain is one of the first organs to die. Again, this is by deliberate design so that the soul of a person can be released quickly when life in the physical body is at an end.

I try to move away from religious terms when describing our soul. My preferred description is that we are a "Conscious Energy". Our soul is made of this energy and the dimension of Heaven is that of Conscious Energy.

The spiritual dimension of Heaven is one where the energy of love is at its greatest natural state. Love can be just an emotion but in its purest form Love is an energy. The dimension of Heaven is almost infinite. The opposite to love is negative energy, or in its worst form it is described as evil. Negative energy is earthbound and exists in small, localised pockets.

There are many different types of spiritual beings in the dimension of Heaven. We can describe them as Angels, Guardian Angels or Spirit Guides. Sometimes I prefer to simply say that "Heaven" helps us in our daily lives.

CHAPTER ONE

Learn how Heaven Helps Us

In order to picture Heaven in our minds it is important that we learn to Visualise through our Third Eye. This not a physical eye, it is our spiritual eye.
When we see images in our mind then these can be memories that have been stored by our brain and re-created as images.
If I said to you "Visualise a place where you went on holiday", then you might see an image of that place in your mind's eye. The image would have been retrieved from the memory in your brain and brought instantly to the front of your mind.

Such images can also be perceived in our soul memory. I know this because every time I give someone an Angel messages reading, bringing-in a loved one who has passed, the Angels give me images of almost anything they wish to communicate. These images would have been captured in the soul memory of the person in Heaven whilst they were in life, and the images are still held in their soul memory in the Afterlife.

If we allocate some time for ourselves to stop occasionally and blank our thoughts through meditation, then we might allow our third eye to pick up random spiritual images.
This is a time we should deliberately not allow ourselves to think about the past, present or future. Importantly, to try to stop

worrying about things for a while.

We will then be hoping that spiritual images might be given to us. Of course, random spiritual images might not appear in our mind. After all, why should any image appear when we are struggling to quieten our thoughts? Our brain is responsible for bringing to the front of our mind our own images and worries. This constant series of images and worries seem to be generated by the brain as a survival mechanism. The survival mechanism constantly reminds us not to forget and be continually reminded of things we need to do. When we pass to Heaven at the end of Life's days we become free of our brain and this allows a wonderful sense of calm and peace, now free from worries and stress. If we can temporarily blank our minds of worry then we become nearer to our true spiritual soul state of existense.

Since I became clairvoyant, I have always blanked my mind of thoughts before I do a reading for someone. I blank my own thoughts completely and leave myself open to whatever my Angel Guide places in my mind. It could be an image of a deceased person who has a love connection with the person I am reading, or a place, or an item of clothing, or anything. I would also, at the same time, receive messages that accompany the image as a sudden "Knowingness".

I will give some examples of how images might be given to me in my Third Eye:

If I am giving someone an Angel messages reading, it is usually to connect with a loved-one who has passed. In these readings I would be given images by my Angel Guide, who will be working with the Guardian Angels of the person sat in front of me, and the Guardian Angel of the person in Spirit. The first image I usually see is the image of the person who has passed. Often, they appear at the side of the person I am reading. I am free to scan up and down the vision of the deceased person. I will usually start by describing whether I am seeing a male or female, old or young, with an approximate age. I can see their hairstyle, hair colour, and their face. I would see if they wore much make-up, and also describe dress jewels such as a ring, or necklace.

I am often drawn to what they are wearing, and the colour and style of their clothing. Sometimes this can be comical, and the humour will be from the person in spirit who might admit to having worn the same slippers for many years, hence they seem well worn. I have had men in spirit deliberately show me an image of holes in their socks. This would have been true to life, and a genuine attempt by a person in spirit to reassure that the Afterlife of Heaven is not doom and gloom, but a place where we can retain a sense of humour. Indeed, the clairvoyant readings consistently show that we retain our character in Heaven. This is because we are all unique, and our character is not just our brain, but our inner being of soul that we call "Me" or "I".

Angel Message Readings

When I give a personal life situation reading it differs from a mediumship reading in that the person in front of me doesn't want to connect with a loved one who has passed. He or she is wanting to know if I can see what is happening in their life, and what can I tell them concerning their future. Again, my Angel Guide works with their Guardian Angels to give me messages that are relevant. I would be be given messages and visions that mean nothing to me, but when I describe what I see are of importance to the person in front of me. I am also given knowledge as a "Sudden Knowingness", and I often hear words, especially names. I tell the client what I see and hear, and the reading will often progress from there.

When I say "Progress", I mean that I sometimes see images of their future, and receive messages concerning their future.

When a client has told me nothing, except to confirm what I say, they are usually amazed about things I describe concerning their past and present life. However, I often tell them "Look, you have come to see me because you want to know what the future holds. Yes, I am clever when I tell you about your past and present when I knew nothing about you, but you already know your past and present, so it is only worth seeing me if I can tell you about your future".

FORTUNE TELLING

It seems amazing when a person with Psychic gifts gives a Fortune Telling Reading. We might think to ourselves "How do they do it".

An acquaintance of mine, a man aged in his sixties is a well-known psychic with a big following. He works in the UK and internationally. He was born into the life of a Gypsy. At the young age of seven his Gypsy parents made him work doing Fortune Telling. The only tuition he got was one instruction: "Just say what comes into your head".

He has given some amazing readings all his life since that young age. In his adult years he spent much of his time in the army so was well disciplined.

In my spiritual research I question "How do such amazing thoughts come into the mind of a psychic?"

The answer is, of course, that someone is helping them. Most psychics would readily agree that it is their Spirit Guide who helps them. I personally know these guides as "Angel Guides", and that is how I will describe them.

You, the reader, might say "How come I don't have an Angel Guide?". Well, the truth is that we all have Guardian Angels with us throughout our life. Some Guardian Angels specialise in Guiding us. Others specialise in channelling healing to us.

The exciting news is that you might learn to connect with your own Angel Guide. In the following narrative I will explain how to understand this. This might not make you clairvoyant but help you discover that our Guardian Angels communicate through our feelings and intuition.

Fortune Tellers are psychics who have some ability to see the future if they are genuine. People might want to know what the future holds for their love lives, family relationships, health, wealth and career.

Mystics who see premonitions of the future have long been viewed as eccentric, yet often over time some of their predictions came true.

In my view it is a time, a new era, where clairvoyant visions, predictions and premonitions can be experienced by many more people. Those in Heaven constantly try to help us.

Our own Free Will is commonly understood to have led us to where we are today and defines our actions and future Life Events. My research has surprisingly led to the conclusion that future events on our Life Plan will happen irrespective of our daily free will decisions.

Free will certainly influences our daily routine. Yet, we can sacrifice some of our free will to another person when in a close relationship with them. We can sacrifice some of our free will by caring for someone and helping them in everyday tasks.

The Future is linked to the Past

The key discovery in my understanding that Heaven knows some of the future was when I came to the realisation that much of our future life is determined and planned in the past. What has been planned for us is then steered into actually happening in very powerful spiritual ways to become our future reality.

However, this process is frequently prevented by our individual spiritual free will. If we don't understand, if we don't want to listen to spiritual guidance from Heaven, then the good positive things planned for our personal future might not happen. Life then becomes a struggle that can last for many years, or even a lifetime.

The heading "Aspects of the Soul" explains in detail how we

might receive guidance from Heaven, namely in the form of our Guardian Angels trying to help and guide us.

How was our future life planned? I call this process simply determining a "Life Plan". Our Life Plan seeks to remedy things that we need to correct, and to give us the opportunity to learn to enable our further spiritual development.

Past Lives

The discovery of First Heaven gave me a realisation that we all have many lives as a human being. The reason for this is so that we hopefully grow spiritually to be more caring and loving to others, and be less self-centred. People who live lives where they hurt others will not grow, efffectively taking several steps backwards in their spiritual development.

Most of us will have experienced life as another person prior to our present life. The person that we truly are inside, the "I" or "Me" has been shaped by previous lives. This "Shaping" contributes to our character and our driving forces in this life.

Firstly, it is essential that we identify our Driving Forces. We can ask ourselves questions such as: "Am I adventurous or shy? Am I outgoing or not? Do I enjoy challenges or not? Am I outspoken?"

Secondly, we need to accept that we have a Life Plan, which was determined in Heaven before we were born. We all have a Life Plan that our Guardian Angels know. We need to identify our Life Challenges that were included in the Life Plan.

What was planned for our future can often be perceived by taking seriously the inner visions of who we always wanted to be, and our inner thoughts of what we always wanted to do.

CHAPTER TWO

ASPECTS OF THE SOUL

LEARN TO RECOGNISE HOW OUR GUARDIAN ANGELS WORK

Discovering how to sense your Guardian Angel can change your life forever!
It opens the possibility of your dreams coming true!
You can be helped towards better health, fewer times of depression, life fulfilment, and a whole new energy and enthusiasm for life!
As a first step in learning about Guardian Angels it is important to learn about "Aspects of the Soul".

Our Behaviour In Life
When we try to determine why people behave as they do, we have the medical science of psychology.
When we try to determine a person's behaviour spiritually, we can identify that behaviour is frequently linked to our relationship with our own Guardian Angel. This relationship is governed by three major aspects to our soul:

Our Higher Self
Our Middle Self
Our Lower Self

Middle Self

I have started to explain Middle Self first because most people live in this Aspect most of the time. The Middle Self is the Centre of our Aspect Being. We may describe this as self-centred behaviour. We have to be self-centred in terms of ensuring our ability to survive in life. This means making sure we have enough food, clothing, and somewhere to live. Heaven understands this. However, our self-centred desires often go further than acquring our basic needs.

In modern, materialistic society our souls are constantly groomed into resonating with the Aspect of the Middle Self. Advertising is everywhere we turn, internet, radio, tv, newspapers and magazines. Our physical brain brings sensations through sight, sound, smell, taste, touch, and desire for positive physical experiences and adventures. Our soul resonates in what we think is a "Normal" way with Middle Self. We are swamped with advertising messages of how we can acquire the material things we desire.

The modern materialistic world is in reality not the normal human experience if we go back in the past to see how human beings lived in simpler times.

It can be seen that the human soul is groomed by society into choosing the Middle Self Aspect. This is our Free Will choice, that our Guardian Angels have to respect, yet it means that our we, our soul, may not resonate in the Higher Self as often as we should.

Lower Self

There are several Spiritual Aspects within the Lower Self. Our Lower Self is primitive, aggressive, survival self:

Many people living in their Lower Self Aspect may have very little conscience. They are capable of hurting people psychologically, and physically. They don't often feel compassion and will cause suffering with no ability to "Put themselves in others' shoes to see how others feel". They enjoy controlling others, especially people who are in a close relationship with them. They drain the energy of people close who are trying constantly to please them.

Another Aspect of Lower Self can be seen in people who constantly feel self-pity. The "Poor Me" syndrome. These people have one thing in common with those previously described in (1) in that they drain the energy of people who are close to them.

An important aspect of Lower Self is where society forces and grooms people deliberately to resonate part of their time in their Lower Self. One example is that of soldiers in wartime situations. They are groomed by their training to resonate in the aggressive survival self, yet in their personal lives would move back their Soul Aspect to resonate in their "Normal" Middle Self, and sometimes in their Higher Self. Guardian Angels may, or may not, still be close to people in these situations. The reasons become extremely complex.

Living in our Lower Self Aspect, if it is by our own Free Will choice, leaves us left cut-off from our Guardian Angels. We may live a life in stress, and constant anger, or depression. We may gain physical advantages over others for a time and acquire short term success over others. We also are at high risk of negative energies taking over our soul.

Higher Self

When we live in the Aspect of our Higher Self we are capable of giving and showing love and compassion for others, and for animals and nature. We might put the interests of others ahead of ourselves.

The absolute Attribute to resonating in the Higher Self is to be able to feel and project Unconditional Love. We will then be "In Tune" with Heaven.

I personally deliberately live and resonate within my Middle Self most of the time. It keeps me grounded, and functioning in the real world and society we live in. When I need to help someone with Angel messages, I connect to my Higher Self by firstly moving my thoughts to feel and project unconditional love. This moves myself into the Higher Self Aspect of closeness with my Guardian Angel, and I receive visions and messages through a direct channel to Heaven.

Most people are capable of moving themselves for short periods into the Higher Self. If you see a baby, or a kitten or puppy, you will notice how you may feel unconditional love... and this is an intense feeling that momentarily might leave you feeling "Better" because you started to resonate in your Higher Self.

GUARDIAN ANGELS CONNECT WITH OUR HIGHER SELF

We all have Free Will to choose whether we live in the aspect of our Higher Self or choose to dwell in our Middle or Lower Self Aspects.

However, we can only know a true connection with our Guardian Angels when we choose to live in the Aspect of our Higher Self.

Our Guardian Angel is the BRIDGE between Heaven - of Unconditional Love- and the physical world in which we live.
The Healing energies and wisdom of Heaven are made available to us via our Guardian Angels.

How we may learn to Live more in the aspect of our Higher Self

Our soul energy shimmers and resonates at different levels, moving and changing within the different Aspect Levels many times each day. We may exist mainly in the Middle Self, mainly in the Lower Self, or mainly in our Higher Self Aspect.

Human beings can resonate Higher Self by focussing on the spiritual energy of unconditional love. We can achieve this in many ways: by helping and caring for others, through prayer, through building-up rather than breaking down (Have you ever noticed that a house can take months to build, a relationship can take years to build...that is how good and positive things are done. Negative energy can destroy a building, destroy a relationship in seconds).

As we start to spiritually grow, by our own Free Will, to resonate more often in the Aspect of our Higher Self, our Guardians will naturally be closer to us, and we will FEEL their closeness

1)   We will not feel that cold, insecure feeling inside, but instead a gentle warmth of love, of inner confidence and spiritual strength

2)   When we are helping others, or doing something good and positive, we will find a new energy to get through the work we need to do. This energy is channelled from our Guardian and is especially noticeable when we are otherwise tired. When we help others or help animals, nature or the environment we will be resonating in Higher Self if our soul is truly loving and caring. This state of Higher Self is also a state of being In Tune with Heaven and brings associated gifts of healing and seeing some of the future. Charity work or any kind of help we offer brings healing to a situation where there is suffering. Also, the ability to see the future if no help was given, and the ability to change the future for the better if help is given.

3)   Our Guardian works through our feelings to bring healing and calm into situations

4)   In some people who are dedicated to truly helping others their Guardian works so closely with the Higher Self, that their energies meld to the point where that person is almost an Angel

5) Living in the Aspect of our Higher Self we may no longer feel depressed

6) Living in the Aspect of our Higher Self means that we can experience our Guardians giving us messages through our FEELINGS, INTUITION, and CONSCIENCE

7) Our Guardians know our basic positive Life Plan. We may be given "Insights" into our future Life Plan through pictures in our soul-mind

8) In our Higher Self Aspect we can keep tunnel vision in what we really want in our future, and our Guardian Angels will put things in place to make our dreams come true, other than winning money!

HOW THE ANGELS HELP PEOPLE

I want to explain how the Angels try to speak to us through our intuition which is the starting point of how they communicate. In the most extreme form, intuition becomes Clairvoyance, but very few people are clairvoyant. Most people know what I mean when I talk about intuition, and many are capable of acquiring some clairvoyant ability. Clairvoyance is actually *a series* of spiritual GIFTS, that we might acquire as we develop spiritually in a positive way. We all have different spiritual gifts, and I hope that many people will learn how Angels communicate with us.

When I receive Angel messages my Angel comes in to give me the clairvoyant ability. People in my audience often comment that they sense a calm, healing atmosphere. My Angel Guide shows me a vision of those who are spiritually very much alive in Heaven, and will pass on messages to loved ones. I also am shown images of places and objects that may mean something to the person I am reading. I may also see what has happened, and what is happening in the lives of those whom I read, and ask my Angel to show me the Life Path for that individual, to help them back on the correct path to fulfilment and happiness.

In addition to bringing messages from those who have passed

across to Heaven, and also "Psychic" readings I can also pick up a lot from haunted buildings and places. Later in this book I will give accounts of some of my experiences in dealing with this type of phenomena. Hauntings are created by negative spiritual energies that are not from Heaven. I am always helped by my Guardian Angel.

Angels Try to Help Us

Angels try to help in the following ways:

Angels speak to us through our intuition. Have you ever struggled with a problem, unable to find an answer, then suddenly the answer is there? Have you ever been overwhelmed by stress and worry, and then somehow you work through the situation? Have you ever had a gut feeling that you shouldn't go somewhere, and later discover that you are glad you listened to your intuition? ….or maybe you didn't listen to your intuition and regretted doing something? Your Guardian Angel helps you through your intuition. There is no language, just an instant awareness of what we should or shouldn't do by a form of telepathy which we don't acknowledge because we don't realise that we are being helped. In some people the fine tuning of their intuition can lead to an individual becoming in some ways clairvoyant. If we pray to God for healing, then a Healing Angel will help bring healing directly to the person suffering, both spiritually, and through those working to help medically.

Angels can be with us to give us STRENGTH. Both physical, and emotional strength.

A Prayer to God is essential. Angels can be with us to guide us through life's problems and difficulties.

Angels helping us in our daily lives can only be appreciated if we believe in God and the Angels.

A word of caution. Angels rarely communicate as a voice in your head unless to give a sudden warning of imminent danger. A voice in your head is not allowed because a voice telling us what to do would go against our "Free Will" to live our lives as we choose. Also, an Angel of God would never be a nuisance by bothering you in ways you don't want. Angels of God certainly never guide us with bad thoughts.

How can a belief in Angels and Heaven help you?

If you can find somewhere quiet where you can spend a few minutes on your own. It could be just another room in your home. Sit quietly, relax, and try, just try to blank your mind and think of nothing for just one minute. What can you achieve by worrying about the past or future? So, sit quietly and try to appreciate the intensity of the moment of "Now". Listen to any background sounds even in the quietness. Did you succeed? Remember, just no thoughts for one minute. In Heaven, time does not exist. There is only the "Now". Time is purely a physical thing....the revolution of the Earth, the hours in the day, the days in a year. We should learn to live more in the moment of the "Now", and appreciate every moment of your life as a gift from God................even in the hardest of times.

Right, now as you sit quietly think about your most pressing problem at the moment. Quietly say a prayer to God, or think a prayer in your mind, and ask for help. Then, leave it at that...............you have passed your problem up to God. Within minutes, hours, or a day or so you may be surprised how suddenly you become aware of an answer to your problem. Alternatively, you may just feel better about yourself, and the problem will be something that you find the strength and wisdom to handle.

This "Sudden answer" is real help from your Guardian Angel. So how has the Angel communicated? Well, by helping you, the feeling of being helped, the intuition that you receive. Sensing your Guardian Angel gives greater certainty that there is life after death. This helps us personally handle grief from bereave-

ment in a better understanding. We can never get over bereavement, yet we can get through it. It helps us see that our own life is just part of an eternal process of the life of your soul. Our soul is the bit inside of you that you know as "I" or "Me".
Angel messages can help people with problems in their lives including problems with finances, relationships, stress, ill health, worry, insecurity, lacking in fulfilment.

I find it easy to see some things in the future for a person that I am giving a reading. However, while these things I see are always good, positive things that a person would want, I realise that the same person might still be going through life difficulties, things going wrong in their life that seem terribly unfair.

When I am given visions of a person's future, images appear in my mind's eye. The mind's eye can also be called the "Third Eye". The images appear in a way that is familiar to all of us. For example, if I say "Visualise "Big Ben in London", even though you might have never been there, you will have seen photos or video of Big Ben, and an image might appear in your mind.
I frequently receive images of the future of things that are not familiar to me, but absolutely relate to the person I am reading. It could be a new home, a new car, or an image of a person whom they are yet to meet in a new friendship. It could be a place they might travel, a new job, or success in sport, or artistic achievement.
The images come into my mind easily, but some fortune tellers might use visual aids such as cards, a crystal ball, or even reading tea leaves!

Spiritual Energies In Nature

When out walking I often see flashes of light, especially in woodland and near streams, rivers and lakes. The Angels are constantly trying to maintain nature, and I see their light energies as they intensify when bring in healing to trees, plants, animals and birds. I can understand why folklore legends of fairies and other mythical creatures exist as some people may have seen the same flashes of light.

Spiritual Energy controls nature. Migrating birds "Know" where to go as they travel many thousands of miles because intelligent spiritual energies guide them. Homing pigeons are guided in the same way. Scientists believe that these birds are guided by the magnetic field, as used in a simple compass. The Earth's magnetic field only work North to South, not fully 360 degrees as would be necessary to use it for guidance.

CASE STUDIES

An Angel reading that connects with a loved one who has passed, can change a person's future

I gave a reading to a lady called Anne. I had never met her before, and she appeared to be aged in her early seventies. The only question I asked is for her name, and then I asked her to say nothing, except to confirm or otherwise the things I would describe.

I immediately saw a lady in spirit whom I knew to be her mother. She was stood, as they usually do, to the left side of Anne. I described her mother's hair. It was grey, not coloured, and curly. This is where I am not very good at description because I don't know the names of different hairstyles. I told Anne my vision and I said "It looks like her hair was nicely kept, and "Permed". Anne smiled for the first time and confirmed what I was seeing. "She is wearing a dark blue cardigan and black skirt". "That will be her, she often dressed exactly like that" said Anne.

I then heard the name "Dorothy" spoken into my mind. "I have the name Dorothy" I said. Anne confirmed: "Yes, that was my mother's name".

A vision then appeared in my Third Eye of her mother in bed, very sick, with Anne caring for her. I heard the words "Please thank her". I relayed the message to Anne that she had to care for her mother. I knew instantly that this had meant that Anne had to live with her mother towards the end of her mother's life. I said to Anne "I can see that you sacrificed a lot to live with your mother to care for her. She thanks you for that". Anne began to show emotional tears, and was overwhelmed in a happy way to receive the message of thanks. I then saw a vision of a locket, holding a photo of her mother. I described the locket to Anne and she pulled it out from where it was hidden behind her coat. It was exactly as described. I went on to give more detail that her mother communicated to me.

At the end of the reading Anne told me how she had previously held no beliefs in a life after death. She had felt insecure and cold inside following the recent death of her mother. Her life, her future, was changed for the better. She knew absolutely that no-one could have given her the information that came through the reading. She knew it was her mother. She would no longer carry the heavy weight of grief. She could move forward with her life feeling better.

Here is a case where a lady age around thirty years was able to see a brighter future following her reading:

Leanne came to see me. She seemed quite happy and bright. When I give a reading my first thought is "Do they want a mediumship reading to connect with a love-one who has passed, or do they want a psychic reading concerning their life issues?" I never ask them this question. My Angel Guide usually points me in the right direction quite rapidly.

In this case it was a psychic reading. I saw that she was no longer in a relationship with a partner, and that she had two young children. As I began to tell her, Leanne confirmed that as correct. Suddenly I saw a vision of her being mentally and physically abused and attacked by her ex-partner, and that this had happened on a regular basis. This was quite a dramatic vision, and as I relayed and described this to her, she confirmed that this was exactly how her relationship had been. She had escaped her relationship in fear of her life.

"It isn't over yet" is what I told her. "Your ex-partner is still making threats to personally harm you". That is correct" she said. "I have a Court Injunction that states he cannot come near my house, but he is so violent that it sometimes doesn't stop him trying to get to me. I need to move home, live somewhere that he can't find me"

I then moved the psychic reading into the mode of seeing the future for her. I saw a new man in her life. A very caring person. I described him in detail starting with his hairstyle and hair colour, the shape of his face, his stature, and the clothes he might typically wear. Leanne had a look of amazement as she opened-up a photo on her phone. "Is this him?" she asked. The photo was exactly the image I could see in my vision. She was astonished at my description of this new man and felt she might start to trust this new relationship that she had found. I then told her that he had been in a relationship that had failed, and that he had one child, a daughter, with shared custody with his ex. She confirmed this.

I concluded the reading by describing a vision of her spending her future life with him, much happier, and able to move away from her current location. I gave her a warning that this new man could be prone to being quiet and moody after finishing work, and that he is quite serious in his work as a baker. Leanne laughed and said that she could cope with that.

At the end of the reading, she expressed amazement at how I could have known the information that I had given her. She felt that her fear and reluctance to move on with her life could now be worked through, and that she could gradually, step by step, move forward in her new relationship.

ROBERT MASON

How does Heaven See Us?

In our understanding the Spiritual Realm of Heaven it can be helpful if we have a clearer picture of how those in First Heaven look upon ourselves as human beings.

The following is a fictional account of how Guardian Angels might see us, and work in helping us. The central character is a Guardian Angel called "M". Although Guardian Angels have no male or female orientation I write about "M" as female. The Angel visions and messages I have received over many years have helped me create this story which for me is just one picture of the reality of how the Angels help us from the Spiritual Realm.

"M" had lived through many lives on Earth as a human being. The Wise Ones in the Spiritual Realm of Heaven now judged that she no longer needed another physical incarnation as a human being. She was ready to become a Guardian Angel, helping people in life with all her experience. Some Guardian Angels are advanced spiritual beings who have never seen life as a human being, and some are souls who have graduated to Angel status having lived many Earthly lives.

The soul energy of M had gradually become a deep shade of purple as she had spiritually grown through each life. New, younger souls start with a white energy that will grow through many earthly lives, and gradually assume visibly deeper shades through spiritual colours similar to yellow and blue as their soul energy gains more knowledge, wisdom and empathy.

During her final life on Earth M had made huge personal sacrifices in helping and caring for others in a hospital. When she eventually fell ill and died her soul energy was tired, and in need of a rest. There is no time in the Spiritual Realm but her soul energy eventually recovered and she began to take on a beautiful radiance of Divine Energy as she prepared for her new role of Guardian Angel.

HEAVEN IS REAL

There are no wings on Angels. Perhaps, because they appear to come from a height in mid-air when seen by people, the artists of old and modern times assume they must have wings. Their radiance shows as a beautiful shimmering energy around them which might be observed and thought of as Angelic wings.

M was given a human soul to look over and guide. The person she would guide would probably not be aware of this once born into physical life.
Before each person enters life, before they are born, a Life Plan is worked out for them. The Life Plan includes the Life Challenges that a person would have to endure. Challenges are not meant to be a time of suffering but work that person will do that achieves something positive.
The Life Plan will also include people who are important to our life that we will meet, including people we will have as family and friends, work that we will do, and interests such as sport, music and art.

The first person that M had to look over was called Ann.
M had spent time with her before her birth. There had been much to do as Ann was given a Life Plan and made aware of some of the Life Challenges she would have to work through. In a previous life Ann had been very self-centred. She had put her own personal needs and wants over those of the three children she had mothered. Her primary Life Challenge for a new life ahead of her was to learn to show more empathy towards others, incuding family.
M had accompanied the soul of Ann as she looked down from Heaven to choose her new parents. Yes, we can choose our future parents, with direction from our Guardian Angel.
Ann had been given a Life Plan that gave her the opportunity to be a healthy child and attend a good school. She had chosen parents who were not wealthy but together her parents earned

enough to support a family because her father worked in a factory and her mother worked as an office clerk.

Ann's Life Plan was to be good at school studies, pass exams with better than average grades and move onto college or university to study towards becoming a veterinary surgeon. Heaven had planned for Ann to work with animals so that she could learn how to become more caring.

M accompanied Ann through her birth into life. At the time of birth Ann's memory of Heaven was deliberately blanked. It is not good to remember who we were in previous lives because some memories might be painful. Also, memories of Heaven would distract us from living our new life as a human being.

During the early years of Ann's life M had helped bring healing to Ann when she was unwell.

Ann was a soul who did not show empathy to others and one day at school she was with her friends who then started to pick on a disabled girl by calling her names and laughing. M tried to get through to Ann via her conscience and M knew that Ann was aware of this. It did no good as Ann ignored her conscience and continued to humiliate the disabled girl.

Many times through childhood M would try to get through to Ann to show more empathy to others but to no avail.

Ann didn't achieve high grades in school or college so was unable to learn to be a veterinary surgeon. However, deep in her mind she knew she wanted to work with animals. M tried to speak to Ann through her intuition. This, at last, seemed to work as Ann responded to her intuitive feelings by volunteering to work at a pet rescue sanctionary. At last Ann was learning to care for something beside herself. She learnt to care for sick animals and nurse them back to health.

In her personal life Ann eventually met someone and married. The marriage was fraught with arguements because her husband was also self-centred. However, together they had a child, whom they thought was a healthy son. However, at the age of 10 months her son showed signs of learning difficulties. Her son became hard work, needing attention most of the time. Ann could no longer work at the animal sanctionary and went through her own internal battles, now having to sacrifice her own needs for those of her son. M tried to work with Ann every day by showing her the best way forward through her intuitive feelings. It was difficult for M, but amazingly progress was made. Ann started to show care and love towards her son.

One of the Life Challenges set for Ann before birth was to be a mother of a child with disabilty to help her change in a positive way. The plan was to give her the opportunity to spiritually grow by learning to become more caring and loving towards others.

M continued to accompany Ann through her life, trying to guide her on the most positive course and trying to keep Ann on her Life Plan. Ann's Life Plan wasn't fully completed because she never became a veterinary surgeon. Also, she had been quite cruel to others when she was younger. However, some major changes had occurred in Ann's ability to truly love and care for her child, and for animals.

At the end of her life on Earth, as with all of us, Ann's life adventure and experiences were captured on her spiritual record for review by the Wise Ones in Heaven. Ann had grown spiritually and M felt a sense of achievement in her first assignment as a Guardian Angel

CHAPTER THREE

Premonitions

I have now experienced many instances where I have been given visions and messages from Heaven concerning the future. This could be a vision of a future for a person I am clairvoyantly reading, or a premonition concerning a future local, national, or world event. Because everything I do and see is then linked back to my logical research, I believe that it is the correct moment in time to explain this to a wider audience. I believe that the knowledge could make the world a better place as more people seek to learn the enlightenment that can be revealed through this knowledge.

This isn't religious, nor an ancient secret kept for millennia. It isn't weird or spooky. This knowledge is simply for any rational person to explore without strings attached.

Premonitions concerning happenings in the world

Unlike visions that I am given by the Angels concerning a person's future, premonitions are given to me unannounced, and without prior thoughts of the events in the premonition given to me.

Premonitions work for me in two ways:
1) If a person I am in contact with is to travel somewhere, I might receive a premonition of any serious weather, natural catastrophe, or other personal danger. I also experience such premonitions for myself.
2) I am constantly experiencing premonitions of global events. I was told by my Angel Guide that something big would affect the entire world in 2020. The "Something Big" turned out to be the COVID-19 Pandemic. Climate Change, and the consequences to nature, and our planet is on the minds of many people, and the subject of many of my premonitions.
I might receive a premonition of a danger if someone I know is to travel to a place, or country.

The following examples are all true accounts of premonitions that came true:

Tsunami

I had a vision of the Boxing Day Tsunami of December 2004. I warned a family member not to travel to a beach resort in Thailand because of my visions of a huge wall of water from the sea overwhelming the coastline and going inland. I didn't know what a Tsunami was, but just saw a huge wall of water. My family member fortunately, for several reasons, cancelled her planned travel to that area. She and her husband had spent months training to be diving instructors and planned to work for a year as diving instructors for tourists at a holiday beach resort in Thailand. Her friends, husband and wife plus a son age four, had made the same plans, and did journey there. When the tsunami hit the man was diving underwater, and was swept four miles down the coast, but was uninjured. The woman saved herself and her son by running inland, and she held her son above her head as the water reached shoulder height. Fortunately, they were not injured.

I also receive such premonitions of danger when I travel:
Bus on fire
February 2018, I had to travel home by bus because my car was in a garage for repairs. I was seated on the left side of the bus, and at the next stop I suddenly saw flames rising up at the outside of the window alongside of me. Yet, passengers were getting on the bus, obviously not seeing the flames. The flames were a vision and disappeared as quickly as they came. I didn't know what to do, so I continued my bus journey. Six miles along the road the bus suddenly stopped. The engine at the rear had suddenly blown up, with steam and oil everywhere, but no flames. Fortunately, no-one was hurt.

Messages I hear as a voice

I might occasionally hear a spiritual voice when trying to help someone is emotionally very upset.
The messages come as a clear voice, but with no emotional expression.
The messages communicate a healing and happy outcome within four weeks, or in one month. The predicted outcome is almost unbelievable at the time.
Here is a real-life example:

Again, this true account concerns a family member. It was Easter 2019 when I spent several hours trying to console a family member whose fiancée had just left him. They had been in a relationship for seven years, yet she had refused to share a home with him. The relationship seemed to be finished with phone contact and social media contact blocked. I didn't move into psychic mode, and, as most people, I began to feel drained of energy as I tried for several hours to help him feel better, but without success.

I needed a break so went to the bathroom. Suddenly the voice I hear spiritually, speaking with no emotion into my mind said: "She will be back in his life in a full relationship and sharing a home in one month". I went back to join my family member, who was suffering severe depression. How could I tell him about the message? I plucked up the courage and told him. He knows my psychic gift and believed me. He became less depressed, and more positive than he had been all day. One month to the exact day later it transpired that not only were they back together, but she moved in to share a home with him.

I always trust that inner voice. It is the voice of my Angel Guide, and those in Heaven can see our future.

The following is a further true account of how some may receive premonitions:

I was giving an Angel messages reading to an elderly lady at her home in the city of Hull. I clairvoyantly brought through her father who had been a fisherman on a Hull trawler during his working life. I then brought through a picture of a trawler sinking with loss of life of all those on board. The lady looked astonished and briefly confirmed the facts, but I asked her not to say anything further.

Her father in spirit then showed me a vision of how he had refused to board ship one day. He had felt intuitively that something bad was going to happen to the trawler that he worked on. He went home and the trawler set sail without him, never to be return home again due to severe weather.

The lady confirmed everything that her deceased father had just told me. She then went on to say that he had lived a healthy and

full life before he died of natural causes aged in his eighties.
This account shows clearly how many people can receive intuitive feelings. My research show that these are given to us by our Guardian Angels. Some people listen to these feelings and act on them. Many people don't. In this book I explain how important it is for all of us to start to believe in our intuitive feelings and be guided by them throughout life. This is extremely important in helping us keep safe in times of a pandemic.

CHAPTER FOUR

Climate Change And Covid-19

Throughout 2019 I was receiving spiritual warnings that "Something Big" would have a negative impact on the populations of the world in 2020. I was as always "In Tune" with Heaven, yet they wouldn't tell me exactly what would happen, which of course was COVID-19.
I had also sensed the alarm and concern in Heaven concerning Climate Change and that some world governments were not prepared to take action.

What was coming was to be attributed to human error, yet had been brought about spiritually to slow down excess travel and excesses of waste that were polluting the planet. COVID-19 has done just that.

Climate Change

Burn, burn, burn,
Oil, Gas, Coal, Wood
Burn, burn, burn
Forests, and places where houses stood

Drown, drown, drown
Storms that rarely came before
Air temperatures rise
Precipitation more
Drown, drown, drown
Crops submerged, fields now lakes
Houses flooded
For our mistakes

World industrial machine,
Once a dream
Powers relentlessly on
Answers to none

Our emissions will be zero
Greenhouse gases are the cause
Other countries won't comply
Nation leaders meet, verbal wars

Somewhere in our world
Fossil fuels burn, no control
This will continue for a few
Yet will impact on us all

Burn, until fossil fuel supplies end
Politicians only talk and recommend
Without real action
World climate change won't mend

Can nations stop temperature rise?
Just watching, while a large part of nature dies.

Fossil Fuels

There will be a time when fossil fuels run dry
Climate Change may slow
Too late, planet Earth may die

Many countries legislate low emissions
International agreements, big decisions
Carbon neutral, plastics reduced,
Recycling, clean energy, less fossil fuels used

Other countries will not comply, nor care
Driven by greed
True interests elsewhere
……but not climate change

The ability of the world to stop climate change will be constantly challenged by the countries and individuals who continue to ignore the problem. Well-meaning countries and well-meaning individuals will be able to work towards slowing the changes. However, most people will continue contributing to climate change damage to our beautiful planet Earth and our fragile environment.

The massive use of fossil fuels over the past two hundred years, accelerating in the latter part of the 20th century and into the first part of the 21st century has been the major cause of climate change.

Heaven created our beautiful planet and the Angels in Heaven bring visions of how our way of life continues

to accelerate the causes of climate change

Examples of how we continue to rely on fossil fuels include powering the internet. The internet needs a huge amount of energy, much of it from fossil fuels, to keep it powered. Everything from our banking systems, social and business communication and the entire control of industry and commerce is reliant on the internet.

A new generation of low emission cars seems to be an eco-friendly move, yet the sourcing of raw materials and the process of manufacturing of a car uses many years of fossil fuel energy.

Wind Farms provide renewable energy, yet the manufacture of wind turbines and their installation uses a huge amount of fossil fuels.

Climate Change will only stop accelerating when fossil fuel reserves, especially oil, start to become scarce.

Like naughty school children leaders of industry and governments will reduce the use of fossil fuel energy only when circumstances force them because they become scarce. Oil will eventually become too expensive to extract from more difficult oil fields. The period of huge use and depletion of fossil fuel reserves will go down in future history as the most destructive period to life and the environment in human history.

What can the world do now?
There are many people working positively to publicise and where possible take action to slow down our excess usage of fossil fuels and plastics plus all the other causes of pollution and climate change.
The Heavens created the universe, our precious planet, and all of life. The Angels constantly bring me messages concering how Heaven will intervene to slow down the damage that hunanity is causing. This intervention is happening in many stages over the

remainder of the twenty-first century.

Diary of the Future

The diary is written from messages received from the Angels, but firstly a poem:

The Dream

My dream turned into nightmare,
Thunder rumbling crash
The storm now coming closer
Apprehension, lightening flash

People running in fear
From an enemy they could not see
Mowed down by serious illness
How, ever could this be?

Our democratic government
New laws police, military
Taking away our freedom,
Destroying jobs,
Our liberty.

I awake suddenly from my nightmare
Thank goodness, just a dream,
I feel shaken and relieved
All is normal it would seem

Had a shower, ate my breakfast
My ordinary everyday tasks,
Left my home to go to work,
Everyone wearing masks.

Climate change concerns took a back seat as COVID-19 spread

immediate and genuine fear across the world. Countries restricted travel access across borders. Social isolation, and social distancing became a new way of living, although some countries are relaxing such measures.

The measures many Governments have put in place does limit the spread of this incredibly contagious disease.

My premonitions keep showing me how COVID-19 will continue to increase the divide between rich and poor nations.

From a Climate Change perspective, during the height of the pandemic some of the unnecessary travel across the world was temporarily shut down. Many industries found it difficult for their business to fully operate. Pollution was slightly reduced. During the summer of 2020 many people commented on how the sky appeared as a deeper shade of blue because of less pollution in the atmosphere. There was a temporary slowing down of some climate change factors. The world is however still racing towards a future Climate Change catastrophe that will see half of the world population die from starvation before the end of this century. That destructive race is still underway, but hopefully slowed down.

Heaven shows me that there are many reasons why the world population will significantly reduce, but lack of food will be the dominant reason. Modern farming techniques make heavy use of chemical weedkillers that soak into the soil and in turn destroy microbes living within the soil. Plants absorb carbon from the atmosphere and, through their roots, feed the microbes that are in healthy soil. Healthy soil can hold a huge amount of the carbon absorbed by plants from the atmosphere but that is not happening with farming methods employed for mass food production.

Modern farming techniques are heavily dependent on fossil fuels to power machinery, to produce fertilisers and agrochemicals. Once oil supplies start to become difficult to obtain then this will have a major adverse effect on world food production.

The main concern of everyone is in what the future holds, and what actions can be taken by governments, and everyone to avoid the worst scenarios, and protect animal life, nature, and humanity for the future.

Known economically usable oil reserves are less than 50 years. This means that at some point in our future diary we should consider building into our picture the slowing of global temperature increases and an estimate of how much damage to planet Earth will still suffer as a direct result of the further global warming until temperature stabilisation.

Heaven is aware and scientists already know that to tackle climate change we will need to change the way that populations of countries run their whole way of life.

Depletion of oil reserves will obviously impact directly on transport necessary for food supplies to be distributed, also impacting massively on manufacturing, and far

It is not good enough to say that "We will all have electric cars". Each electric car produced uses 15-30 years of fossil fuel in its manufacture. Oil is used in modern farming methods, the growing of crops and food production.

A country with significant investment in wind turbines and solar power can be more innovative in change than a country that does not invest.
In the manufacture of wind turbines many years of energy is used in their manufacture and installation. That means that a turbine needs to operate for many years before it becomes carbon neutral. It has to generate free energy for a considerable period of time before it starts to generate energy above and beyond the fossil fuel energy used in its manufacture.

21st Century Predictions

Heaven is Real and the incredible creative intelligence in Heaven is working to save humanity and our planet Earth. However, much of this has to be actioned by humanity which means that as many people as possible need to believe in Heaven and understand that our Angels are trying to guide us. Governments have long since woken up to the damage being caused to nature and the environment, but some governments are still doing little to move industry away from heavy fossil fuel consumption. Many species of life are on the verge of extinction.

During the years 2025 - 2030 we must continue to educate people on how their lives will change. Heaven wants to help people to fulfil their inner "Calling" to do something positive.

Diary Year 2030

Oil prices soar as major oil producers control supplies in view of concerns over usable reserves.
Heavy rain contrasted by droughts and severe heat become the norm. Many wildlife species in danger in 2020 have now become extinct. Some species held in zoos and other Ark Projects are saved from becoming extinct.

Diary Year 2035

Oil reserves are becoming harder to extract. Many poorer countries experiencing hunger and high death rates. Severe weather events have brought famine to many poorer countries due to crop failures.

Years 2030-2039 will see still some countries still burning vast amounts of fossil fuel.

Many people and countries will be working hard to ensure food production is maintained, and wildlife preserve

Diary Year 2040

The vast majority of commuters are now using public transport. Food production globally is seriously hampered by the high cost of oil. The way of life of people is having to drastically change. The internet becoming unreliable due to power outages affecting web servers. The production of greenhouse gasses peaks around this year. Fossil fuel depletion is reducing the rate of global warming. However, global temperatures now up 2 degrees centigrade compared with pre-industrial, and severe weather events cause crop damage and failures in many countries. Nature and wildlife suffer, and human beings suffer high death rates in poorer communities in all countries.

Premonition: Year 2050 is the "Crunch" year for nature and humanity. Wealthier countries will continue to get by comfortably, but with major lifestyle changes. Climate change acceleration will have slowed because fossil fuels are becoming depleted. The effects of climate change will have made farming no longer possible in some areas of the world. Poorer countries will experience famine on a scale that the Earth has never before experienced. There will be many localised wars, and conflicts.

The decade 2040-2050 will go down in history as the time when modern civilisations were forced by oil shortages to change their ways of living.

Diary Years 2050-2100

The Visions that the Angels give me concerning the latter part of the twenty-first century are perhaps the worst scenario based on Heaven not being able to influence humanity as fully as possible. Tensions globally centre around the impact of global warming on agriculture, plus depleting oil reserves. Governments take action to ensure that food production in farming and that manufacturing are kept going. Countries strive to get things right at a local level.

The years 2050-2100 will see world population shrink by half as food production becomes increasingly more difficult. Localised wars to secure oil supplies. Government control of gas and coal reserves by countries that own these. We must continue to adapt our lifestyles.

Nature in plants, tree and animal species will have seen a severe reduction due to human beings destroying more forests. There will at last be global action across most countries to change the way that we live.

History books in the 22nd century will look back on the 20th and 21st centuries as being the most destructive in the history of humanity.

THE FUTURE OF PLANET EARTH

The spiritual Source, the vast creative intelligence, the reason and purpose for everything, that religions may call "God", is aware of the very real dangers to our beautiful Earth.

The Angels and other advanced spiritual beings work in the purpose of the Source and are working to try to prevent things getting worse.

Lifting the Veil

The prediction of world population halving from almost eight billion to four billion by the end of the twenty-first century means inevitably that we will face human suffering on a scale never experienced before.

During World Wars One and Two many millions perished yet these numbers are nothing compared with the cutting short of lives that will occur later in the 21st century.

Negative energy, in other words evil actions, will become widespread as countries seek to preserve their wealth and lifestyles against a backdrop of hugely diminished food availability and the resources needed to service our modern industrial economies.

When I use the term "Lifting the Veil", I refer to the memory of Heaven that is deliberately blanked off when we are born into our life as a human being. There are many reasons why we are not allowed to retain a memory of Heaven, some of which are explained elsewhere in this book. In April 2021 I received a message from Heaven that the "Veil" of memory recollection of Heaven would be lifted for some people so that they could be aware of how Heaven will guide human beings through the difficult times ahead. Such people will be blessed with true enlightenment.

In order that the negative energy and human suffering ahead can be minimised, alleviated, and a better world be made possible for the future, there will be powerful spiritual forces working in many ways for the good of humanity.

Throughout 2018 and 2019 I was given spiritual warnings that "Something Big" would affect populations around the world in 2020. I wasn't told what the "Something Big" would be, but as we are all aware the COVID-19 pandemic has been just that. Who could have imagined that a pandemic could affect every country across the planet? The pandemic has been a negative event, affecting human populations in an unwanted way. The Lifting of the Veil messages I am receiving are just the opposite. This is spiritual help that will be positive across all countries, across all human populations. The spiritual help will be something never experienced before and considered to be in many ways miraculous.

I don't know the exact detail of how this spiritual help will come about. I am being told that spiritual leaders who show great wisdom and healing gifts will arise across different faiths.

It's seems to be as big as the "Second Coming" of Jesus Christ, yet my logic tells me that a Second Coming won't be recognised by other religions, nor by science, nor even by many Christian churches. I have been given a specific date in the year 2029 for the miraculous happening which, on reflection afterwards, strangely fits in approximation with 2000 years since Christ was most active. The happening is likely to be witnessed in a local community before news spreads further.

There will be spiritual teachers, with the wisdom of teachings from God, that arise in faiths across the world.
Science will make further breakthroughs in discovery that will result in some areas of research being directed to seek scientific evidence of the spiritual dimension. This will help facilitate the belief and acceptance of Heaven.

A female figure will emerge around the year 2050 who will lead many millions of people. She will be sent by Heaven and will be working in the purpose of God. She will play an important part in helping the world through the most difficult years 2050 to 2100. After 2100 the world will be of smaller population, yet still technologically advanced. Humanity will finally be working with nature and the environment rather than causing destruction. This female figure will be named by many as a spiritual "Mother". This will refer to her as spiritual Mother of the age on Earth beyond 2100.
The time of suffering throughout the latter part of the 21st century will also be a time of many miracles.
The Time of Miracles will address the damage to our precious planet Earth and guide and bring healing to populations in many countries across the world.

CHAPTER FIVE

Angels at Work

How Angels Communicate with us

Angels communicate into our thoughts so completely that we may just take them as being our own thoughts. We have free will. Our inner voice might not even be a voice because it is a series of thoughts that try to warn us and guide us. We constantly create our own thoughts, but the inner voice is different in that the thought, and ideas suddenly come from nowhere. I best describe this as a sudden "knowingness".

With free will, we can choose to ignore our inner voice. If we do this frequently enough then we lose our close relationship with our Guardian. We may then become reckless in our actions, and inconsiderate, lacking in empathy for other people, and for animals, nature and the environment.

We may have spiritual gifts such as charity work, concern for animals, concern for nature, concern for the planet. When we balance our free will thoughts with our inner voice from our Guardian then our spiritual gifts will bear fruit. We can and do generate our own love for others, and we have our own skills and abilities.

Guardian Angels are a part of our conscience. Our conscience is within our inner self and may whisper to us that something we have done, or are considering doing may hurt someone, or hurt an animal, or hurt nature.

Some people become so self-centred that they never listen to their Guardian Angel.
In such cases their Guardian is unable to give thought into the minds of these people that act as their conscience. Eventually this cutting off from their Guardian is so total that they no longer hear the inner voice. Their Guardian cannot get through to them. Such people might seem to be civilised and confine their self-centred actions to walking over others legally in business, career, or relationships. They, and others can, and do hurt people physically or mentally without feeling guilty.
Negative, external earthbound spirits of evil energies cannot get inside anyone who has still a connection with their Guardian Angel. Our Guardians protect our inner selves from negative energies. The earth plane does have a lot of negative energy. Also spirits who are evil can still be bound to the earth plane and seek opportunities to target individuals who have torn away from their Guardian. Negative, evil spirits can then try to communicate directly into their thoughts. If such a person has a dark character it is easy for the evil spirit to stoke their fire of self-centred purpose to cause harm. This type of person goes out and does harm to others, and has no conscience concerning harming animals and nature.
Our Guardians work through our intuition, giving sudden answers to problems, feelings inside about what to do. These seem to come from nowhere. An impossible overpowering problem can suddenly be answered by seeing what to do.
Spiritual Gifts... how our Guardian Angels become one, melding with us when we want to use our spiritual gifts. This "As one" feeling may produce a totality of our inner thoughts, and spiritual powers to enable us to do the work, as being OURSELVES

creating the thoughts in our minds.

I firmly believe that many scientific discoveries have been inspired inside the thoughts of our great scientists by their Guardians as part of some Higher Plan.

Our Guardian Angels can also work externally in helping these things around happen in a better way for you.

Our Guardians Angels bring healing. Just think about our fragile body and how it is a miracle we can survive in life.

Angels can help us achieve that deep-down longing for fulfilment that most of us yearn. We all have different talents and ability, and our Guardians can help us make the most of what we have got.
The most successful people achieve their ambitions and personal goals through being totally focused. They have tunnel vision and imagine where they want to be and what they want to achieve. If their vision is good, and will cause no hurt or harm, then they will be helped by listening closely to the inner voice from their Guardian Angel. People are mostly unaware that their own thoughts and visions can be added to by their Guardian, who may feed them ideas, inspiration, motivation and positive energy along the way.
Yes, our Guardians feed us many differing kinds of positive spiritual Energy!

Guardian Angels can sometimes be seen clairvoyantly, especially when their energies are intensified whilst healing someone. They are Beings of Unconditional Love from the Spiritual Realm of Heaven and will never put thoughts in people's minds that will cause hurt or harm in any way.

OUR GUARDIAN ANGELS CHANNEL HEALING TO US

Healing energies from Heaven bring a quicker recovery from illness, to ease the pain of stress or bereavement, and to ease depression.
Healing can be to our lives, to provide a happier and brighter future and personal fulfilment through greater success in whatever we do.

You may think "I don't often need healing, for I am generally in good health".
Alternatively, you may think "I don't have a Guardian Angel healing me, for I am always unwell".
Our Guardian Angels constantly bring healing to us
Our human body is frail in this harsh world we live in. It is a miracle that we can survive with such a fragile body, constantly at risk from injury and accident, and constantly exposed to germs that cause illness.
Many people damage their health through bad diet, smoking, drinking alcohol, lack of exercise. Our Guardian Angels are constantly working to help us when our free will actions are harming our bodies
That miracle is the constant work by our Guardian Angels, healing, protecting, guiding us away from danger, and trying to keep our immune systems, and other bodily defences at optimum efficiency.

LIFE ENERGIES

Our Guardian Angels channel Healing Life Energies into us.
As a clairvoyant, the time when I most often see Angels is when their energies are intensified in channelling healing to other people.

Life Energies can be a shade of purple, pure healing energy, Springtime light green for renewing body cells, and Golden for pure Life Energy, plus many other shades of the colour spectrum.

The following is a true account:
A was giving a lady an Angel Mesages reading, and brought some meaningful messages from her grandma, who had raised her throughout childhood, and had been a loving mother because her real mother had left the family for another relationship. Towards the end of the reading, I picked up that she was in severe pain with her left knee. She confirmed what I said and told me that she was to have a knee operation, to fit a replacement knee, the next day. I asked her if she would like some spiritual healing and she agreed.

When I give healing, it is non-contact. I hold my hand a few centimetres away from a person's forehead and talk through what happens. I immediately saw several healing Angels come in close. One channelled a blue energy to bring pain relief and ease the inflammation around her knee area. Another brought in a Springtime green energy to help renewal of the damaged cells in her muscles and tendons. A beautiful purple energy came in to bring powerful healing to her. I could see the Angels shimmering with the colour of the Life Energies they channelled.

The lady became very relaxed and started to feel well as the pain disappeared.

I saw the lady a few weeks later. She was walking without pain, and excited to tell me that the knee replacement operation had gone exceptionally well, and she had made a recovery much quicker than her surgeon had expected. She commented that she was convinced that this was due to the powerful benefit of the healing she had received from the Angels.

Another true account
I gave a reading to a young woman who was pregnant, but her personal health was damaged by an extremely bad "Junk Food" diet, smoking, drinking alcohol etc. Her baby was subsequently born perfect. I am not a medical person but know enough about the human body to realise that our cells need the correct nutrition, trace elements, proteins, that are the building blocks of life. I am certain many of you reading this will have known a mother with similar lifestyle, although I realise that babies can be born with health problems from mothers who don't take care of their personal health.

I asked my Guardian: "How can the baby have such perfection?"
My Guardian replied: "Through invisible Life Energy the Healing Angels can channel into a baby in the womb the building blocks of Life that people might truly believe can only come from nutrients in food, or from the mother"

Intuition

Guardian Angels work through our intuition, giving sudden answers to problems, and feelings inside about what to do. These seem to come from nowhere. An impossible overpowering problem can be answered by suddenly seeing what needs to be done. *Angels communicate into our thoughts so completely that we just take them as being our own thoughts.*

Conscience

Our Guardian Angels work through our conscience so strongly that my research indicates our conscience may be up to 100% our Guardian Angel.

As human beings we all have the gift of Free Will. It seems that our Guardian Angels cannot prevent us from making our Free Will decisions in everyday life. What they can and do is to put feelings into our minds that we commonly describe as our "Conscience". These feelings are like an inner voice, urging us not to do something that may hurt others.

Many of our actions in life impact directly on others. If our actions in some way cause hurt to others, either emotionally, psychologically, or physically then our conscience should make us aware of this. We may question our conscience and say: "Well, I know a person, or other people may not like what I intend to do, but it is for "Good" in the long-term."

Alternatively we may just go-ahead and do things which hurt others in some way, and our actions are for our own self-centred needs and satisfaction.

Our conscience should always tell us if we are doing something spiritually wrong.

Some people are so self-centred that they always ignore their conscience. Eventually they lose their conscience completely. Their Guardian Angel cannot get through.

Something new starts to happen. When a Guardian Angel has to stand back because someone is totally self-centred and is going through life hurting others, then it leaves a spiritual void. The void is caused because the Guardian Angel has had to stand back, cannot get through and cannot protect the individual from negative, evil energies.

Negative energies are always around waiting on the earth plane, waiting for an opportunity to get into someone who is no longer pro-

tected by their Guardian Angel.
Once negative energy starts to influence a person then their evil actions towards others become more intense and more frequent.

Spiritual Gifts

We all have some Spiritual Gift. It is better not to envy or be jealous about someone else's spiritual gift, but to try to identify our gift, and make the most of it.
We may have spiritual gifts such as charity worker, concern for animals, concern for nature, concern for the planet. When we balance our free will thoughts with our inner voice from our Guardian Angel then our spiritual gifts will bear fruit. We can and do generate our own love for others, and we have our own skills and abilities.
People who have an inner driving force that helps others, or helps nature, or helps the environment can be classed as having a spiritual gift.

Guardian Angels help us when we work to help others

Our Guardian Angel will help us with our work, and at times almost become one with us in terms of spiritual energy and purpose. At such times we will care less about ourselves, other than keeping ourselves healthy, and be almost totally dedicated to the purpose of helping others.

Problems and Guidance

Angels communicate into our thoughts so completely that we just take them as being our own thoughts.

We have free will. Our inner voice is not even a voice but thoughts that warn us, guide us. Don't get me wrong, we constantly create our own thoughts. The inner voice is different in that the thought, and ideas suddenly come from nowhere. I best describe this as a sudden "knowingness".

With Free Will we can choose to ignore our inner voice. If we do this frequently enough then we lose our close relationship with our Guardian. We may then become reckless in our actions, and inconsiderate, lacking in empathy for other people for animals, nature and the environment.

Real Life Examples of how our Guardian Angels Guide Us

Self: "I want to earn a lot of money. I will earn money by becoming a pop star or successful actor"

Guardian: "These are not your talents. Don't try to be something you haven't the talent for."

Focus on what you feel from your Guardian you can do, try hard, and be a success!

Self: "I am out shopping but don't know where to go for a gift for my family member/ friend. I am getting stressed and tired."

Guardian: "Just blank your thoughts, slow down. You will suddenly know which shop to go into and be drawn to a suitable gift." This is your Guardian at work!

A "Calling"

Ever wondered why some people are so determined to do something to help others? Why some people are determined to work helping animals, nature, or the environment?

I believe that many people are given a "Calling". This is a gift from Heaven to do a particular task. The task is part of a Divine Plan to make sure that every aspect of life has people interested in caring and working to cherish, protect, repair and bring healing.

Our Guardian Angels know this Divine Plan and work to help those with a Calling to help them fulfil their inner driving force to care for other people, or care for animals, nature, and planet Earth.
Our Guardian Angels Can Give Us Special Help.

At times we may need special help in life.

For ourselves we may need special healing in times of health crises.
We may need extra help through difficult situations.
For others we may wish for urgent healing when seriously ill or injured. For others we may wish for their lives to be urgently improved from bad situations.

How Can We Ask for Special Help?

We ask for Special Help through Prayer. Yes, prayer either in our thoughts, or out loud. Prayer alone, or in unison and harmony with others.
Our thoughts and prayers are heard in Heaven because Heaven is a place of pure thought.
How do we Pray?
We should never pray to our Guardian Angels. They work in the purpose of God, and on the instructions of God.
We should always pray to God. Pray upwards to the Highest Spiritual Authority, to God, and the powerful, loving actions needed to answer our prayer will be passed back down to our Guardian Angels.

ANGELS HELP US TOWARDS OUR DREAMS OF FUTURE ACHIEVEMENT

Firstly: What is your vision of what you want for the future? Are such dreams positive and good?
Secondly: What talents and abilities do you have? What talents and abilities don't you have?
Thirdly: You can fight through disability. You can fight through being in the wrong part of society. You can fight through lack of academic ability or achievement. You can fight through having no start-up money.
Fourthly: You will find it harder in a society that suppresses people. Your dreams have to be realistic within the society you live.
Our Guardian Angels work through our dreams. Not all the time. When a dream seems REAL then it will be real.
Our Guardian Angels are of the Spiritual Realm and can link our soul to Heaven whilst we are in dream state. This might be to link to loved ones who have passed. I have heard many people tell me how they experienced dreams that seemed like real life with their husband/wife/parents who had passed.

Dreams frequently give us mixed visions of our life events that are difficult to interpret. Our physical brain replays current life experiences, and these can be mixed with spiritual visions from our Guardians.
Dreams are taken seriously by many people.

FREE WILL: THE MOST DIFFICULT PART OF OUR PERSON

Angels stand back when our Free Will is driven by self-centred behaviour that will hurt others.
We are all given a life for a very important purpose. That purpose is to spiritually grow.
Our life on Earth as human beings is a transient experience.
We are in Heaven before we are born, and we return to Heaven at the end of physical life.
We are given life to experience being human. Interaction with others in our relationships with people is a massive part of that experience. We are given life for learning, for adventure, for the physical experiences of walking, running free, sport, and competition.
We seek to find love again, as we experienced in Heaven, where love is the air we breathe. We may find love in our mother's arms as a baby. We seek love in our relationships as we grow older. Sometimes such love can be confusing because it is tainted by desire.
The true unconditional love from Heaven is still with us through our Guardian Angel. If we recognise our Guardian Angel as close to us, then we may feel that love with us most of the time. If we choose by our Free Will to distance ourselves from our Guardian Angel, then we may feel cold and isolated inside.
Free Will is given to us because as spiritual beings we are respected by Heaven.
We can choose to do what we want in life, but often our Free Will urges may knock us off the path of our Life Plan. Things go wrong and we wonder why.
The most destructive parts of Free Will become apparent when

we choose to ignore our Guardian Angel. Many of the populations of the world are not even aware of their Guardian Angels, so Free Will choices are made without this high level of awareness. Often, we find people acting in a self-centred way, not caring too much if they hurt others emotionally, psychologically, or physically.

Through their Free Will many people inadvertently or deliberately go against all the ways their Guardian Angels try to Guide them. These ways are through a person's conscience, intuition, and caring thoughts. On far too many occasions Guardian Angels are forced to stand back, for such is the gift of Free Will that we are allowed to prioritise the decisions we make for ourselves, even when we cause harm.

Negative energy is not far away in all our lives. The world is constantly generating all kinds of spiritual energy from the vast amount of spirits in the form of living people that are currently in life.

Love is the strongest, most powerful energy of all, constantly battling against the negative, evil energies in our physical universe.
If people, through their Free Will, choose to act in a self-centred way that may hurt other people, or hurts nature or the environment in a big way then their Guardian Angel cannot get through. The tragedy is that negative entities might then see an opportunity to get through into the minds of these people. This makes their self-centred behaviour move in the direction of evil. This is a big subject!

I can describe to people I read through clairvoyant visions of their personal future, but with the ability to help them change their future to be happy and fulfilling. This is an important factor because we all have the ability to change our futures when we learn to recognise and accept spiritual guidance that can be available for us every minute of every day.
Guardian Angels are working through many, many people via

their intuition, to give them a "Calling" to help during a pandemic, and longer-term to avert the more serious consequences of Climate Change. That is why some people seem extremely dedicated to this work.

We need to educate the world concerning the spiritual guidance that can be sought concerning real ways and actions to avoid the serious consequences of climate change.

CHAPTER SIX

Sensing Angels

As a person who can sense Angels I can give readings, and bring Angel messages, concerning someone who has passed, I can give Psychic readings about a person's life, and I can also give "Life Plan" readings about a person's future.
I may see images that are visions of something in a person's future, such as a someone they might meet, a job they might have, an interest or hobby, a place they might travel, a place they might live, plus a vision of wealth, a new car, or other new possession.
I also receive premonitions of the future of our beautiful and precious planet Earth.

As an example of seeing the future on an individual basis the following is a true account of an Angel messages reading that involved seeing the future for a lady. Without her telling me anything beforehand, I discovered in the reading that her family were deeply troubled by what had happened to their son. During the reading I saw two outcomes for their son, one good, and one not so good, so I focussed on the good path, and the future changed as I spoke to become the better outcome.

The lady sitting in front of me screamed. Her scream shook the house and surely neighbours would come running in to see what had happened. I was a stranger who had been sat facing this lady across a kitchen table for no more than five minutes. Her scream shook me with an unexpected shudder of sudden stress because I am not the kind of guy who does anything to make women scream. I am a clairvoyant and she had booked me to visit her home to give her a reading. This lady was aged around 40 years and was obviously taking no care of her appearance with greasy hair all over the place, and scruffy clothes. She seemed depressed as she welcomed me into her house and sat me down.

My first words were simply "It's about Justice – or rather an injustice – your son is in prison for an offence he didn't commit" That is when she screamed. I'd visualised some heavy-weight fighter of a husband appearing and throwing me out, but fortunately she had kicked him out of the house for a few hours for privacy during the reading. What I told her was absolutely correct, but then I went on to tell her that her son's prison sentence would be overturned, and he would be a free man within four weeks. Her scream was of surprise at how I could possibly know all of this. I spent another hour with her, bringing-in some quite clear messages from her deceased mother. She calmed down very quickly and became more optimistic and much happier over that hour, and the messages from her mum appeared to be of great meaning. I left her with good wishes, inside my mind saying a quiet prayer for her and her son.

This was in the city of Hull, which I only visit several times a year, and I never go to the public houses there. However, about a month later I did call into a Hull pub with some friends, but in a different area of the city. Hull is a big place. Within minutes an attractive lady came running up to me and gave me a big hug saying: "It's him... it's him...". I couldn't help but notice a rather tough looking partner behind her looking quite angry at her behaviour. "It's ok," she told him. "This is the clairvoyant". The partner changed his mood, put a smile on his face and shook my hand. "Our son is no longer in prison, everything you said came true". The fact that their son was now free was good news, but the added miracle for me was the transformation of this lady. She had taken on a new zest for living, pulled herself out of depression, and acquired a new interest in taking care of herself. She had given herself a makeover with her hair and dress, with such a dramatic improvement that I hadn't recognised her immediately. This was the miracle of what clairvoyance can offer. I have witnessed this miracle many times as people take their lives off "hold" and start living again. My friends in the pub had been staring-on in amazement. I didn't openly discuss my clairvoyant work. One of my hobbies is singing, and we had just done a concert, so my fellow singers in the pub knew nothing about my clairvoyance work. I just tried to shoulder-off what had happened in a joking way.

CHAPTER SEVEN

LIFE PLAN ANALYSIS

As a clairvoyant who connects and works with the Angels I find that people often ask me "Why has my life been so difficult? Why does everything seem to always go wrong for me?"
Of course, a reading doesn't stop an immediate return to the problems and difficulties that someone might live with on a daily basis.
Life Plan Analysis is a deeper way of looking at someone's life.
I have the clairvoyant ability, working with my Angel Guide, of seeing part of a person's Life Plan that was determined in Heaven before they were born. Much of our life was actually planned before we were born, including the challenges and difficulties that were put there to make us stronger and wiser.

LIFE PLAN READINGS ARE MUCH DEEPER

When I am giving someone a Life Plan reading, I am given messages and visions by the Angels and can see if some of the difficulties, some of the things that went wrong, are now at an end. These challenges might have been set in their Life Plan before they were born, but I can see if the times of difficulty are now over. I can also see what life challenges there might be still to come, as well as the good things such as achieving the things a person dreams about, life fulfilment, perhaps meeting the right person for a close friendship, perhaps a job of work, achievement in art or sport, and dreams of where we may want to live or travel. The COVID-19 pandemic and fears for the future concerning climate change have led to many people wondering if they have a future. In this book I explain how, by becoming spiritually more aware, of Heaven and our Guardian Angels, we can keep safe and have a rewarding future.

OUR GUARDIAN ANGELS KNOW OUR FUTURE

When I am giving someone a Life Plan reading my Angel Guide, and my Guardian Angels are working with their Guardian Angels. Our Guardian Angels know our Life Plan and know some of our future.

Heaven won't let us see all of the future. There are good reasons for this, but Heaven will allow us an insight into some of our future.

Guardian Angels have almost always have been many years trying to "Get Through" to the person by trying to guide them by giving them intuitive feelings every step of the way. However, in this modern materialistic world we are told that spiritual things aren't real, including the existence of Angels, so many people never listen to their intuition.

Life Plan Analysis can help change your future for the better!

When I give someone a Life Plan reading some amazing visions unfold before my spiritual eye.

I am usually given two versions of the future, two paths for someone. The first path is a future that would happen anyway, without my intervention. It usually has the same difficulties and challenges that a person has experienced in life up to the present, continuing as before.

The second version of the future is a path of greater happiness, life fulfilment, fewer things going wrong. I choose not to dwell on the first path, so I describe the happier, more fulfilling second path to the person I am giving a reading to.

The miracle is that as I describe the second path it actually changes the person's future for the better. The second happier, more fulfilling path becomes their new future. The reason for this is that our Guardian Angels will put things in place to make our future better if we can believe that to be true.

The moment in time I give an in-depth Life Plan reading is the pivotal moment in a person's life that changes their future for the better!

I have helped many thousands of people free of charge over the past 15 years, by giving them Angel message readings. I am guided by the Angels who work in unconditional love, and I always work using my spiritual gift of Discernment. This is the true ability to discern between good and evil. Opening oneself up to spiritual messages and visions from Heaven is risky because any enhanced spiritual awareness can also open ourselves up to the heavy negative, evil spiritual energies that are earthbound. The ability to discern comes with the knowledge that negative energies can be blocked, instructed to go away, and even dealt with by prayer. I often pray for the Angels that I call "Rescue Angels" to carry away earthbound souls to a place where they can find peace.

In addition to bringing messages from the Angels for people, I also receive messages other from Heaven. These have been given to me over many years.

The messages have revealed an amazing picture of the meaning of life. This has helped me to help others which is absolutely the reason why I have been given this work.

Life Plan Analysis is not just simply knowing what our personal future may become but being aware that we can change some of our personal future to maximise our happiness and fulfilment.

LIFE LESSONS

Our Life Plan was determined in First Heaven before we were born: What we would do, where we would live, people we would form a relationship with, including Soul- Mates.

We may find ourselves making the same mistakes over, and over again. In human relationships, career, personal-finance, and all aspects of our lives. We may be told that is the fault of our Free Will, but often we seem slow to learn. Sometimes the real reason is because of our Life Lessons.

Life Lessons are worked-out and planned before we are born. These can be identified through clairvoyance. Life Lessons can also be identified by recognising the life experience of recurring unfair, difficult times such as in relationship problems.

Once our Life Lessons are identified we can change our outlook on how we tackle the future. Life lessons do not include serious illness or accident. These events are not on our life plan. The way that we can avoid these is to learn to listen to spiritual warnings that we are given through our feelings, primarily our intuition. The way that this works is explained later in this book.

FREE WILL

A lot of weight is given to Free Will steering our lives. It certainly influences our everyday routine decision-making.

We may also be surrendering some of our Free Will to others, such as when we are in a personal relationship.

No matter what our Free Will does for us, or which way it leads us, our positive Life Plan events will still happen.

Future global events such as severe weather events and natural disasters can be seen through clairvoyant visions at a personal level if that person is to travel to the affected area. Warnings can be given to avoid the situation.

Future Personal incidents, that may be seen in a vision as unwanted, can often be prevented from happening by making a prayer to God. The Angels will work to stop them from happening.

SIXTH SENSE

The Spiritual Realm of Heaven is a place of Unconditional Love. We may travel through life worried about the future, and sometimes feeling cold inside, because we are not feeling the love from our Guardian Angels. The society we live in does not teach how to recognise our Guardian Angels. I show people how to re-connect with their spiritual love and guidance that can lead us to true happiness and fulfilment. Many people have a "Sixth Sense" that gives them feelings inside that Heaven and Guardian Angels really do exist.

LOGICAL EXPLANATIONS

Logical discoveries through Spiritual Research are mostly not capable of being proven by science, simply because science, especially physics, is based entirely on the way our physical universe is put together. The Spiritual Realm of Heaven is another dimension, with its own building blocks that cannot be measured by our physics. Both our universe, and the spiritual dimension of Heaven have one major thing in common, and that is immense energy. I personally believe that, just like weighing scales, the energy of our physical universe is in balance with the energy of the spiritual dimension.

FIRST HEAVEN

There are many people who have had "Near Death Experiences" (NDE), and for those who wish further reading there are many books, and YouTube videos where you can see personal stories of such experiences.

As a Clairvoyant, I can see through to the beautiful place that many who have an "NDE" travel to. I call this place "First Heaven". Why? Because it is the first place most of us go when we first leave our Earthly life. It is a very real, solid place, and created in the image of the Earthly home we have just left so that we can transition into the next life. There are valleys, rivers, lakes, trees, flowers, green grass. Colours are vivid and the experience of being in that place is intense and joyful. Others who have passed may be waiting to greet us, but only where there is a bond of love or warm friendship. Dogs, cats, horses, can be seen with those who cared for them in life.

We can stay in this place for a long time, although there is no real time, but only the moment of "Now".

We will then move on to further experiences, and ultimately to be reborn into another life.

REINCARNATION

It would seem that we all have many lives. Each life is given to us for adventure, experience, challenges, and hopefully spiritual growth.

How do we achieve spiritual growth?

We grow spiritually when we become less self-centred, and more caring towards other people, towards animals, nature and the environment.

To spiritually grow is why we have many lives, and our Life Plan is reset before each life to improve on our previous lives. Our Guardian Angels know our Life Plan.

WHO ARE WE?

We are an immortal soul. Our soul energy cannot be seen because it is made of the same stuff as energies within the spiritual realm.

Over many years of giving Angel messages readings, I see that we retain our memories, and our character when we leave our physical body and pass back home to Heaven at the end of our physical life. Our soul, the person we are, the "I", the "Me" inside each one of us is eternal.

What do those in Heaven know about our future?

The Spiritual dimension of Heaven is a place of infinite intelligence. We all have a Life Plan that was determined for us before we were born. Those in Heaven know our Life Plan. Our Life Plan would include the major events planned for our life such as whom we might meet, the work we will do, and the interests we might pursue, plus much more. When fortune tellers pick up future happenings in a person's life these are the things they might pick up. However, other things are also planned for our lives before we are born, and fortune tellers often miss these. I call them "Life Challenges". Such challenges can be hard, difficult, and make life a struggle for long periods of time. They are put in place to give us life experience, adventure, and with a purpose of helping us spiritually grow more rapidly. Spiritual Growth means to become more caring towards others, towards animals and nature, and towards the environment of our planet Earth. Those who have an inner drive, a Calling, to do what they can to reduce the effects of climate change are an example of human beings caring about our planet Earth, and the future of humanity, and nature.

Those in First Heaven are actually living in a place of beauty, unconditional love, purpose, and oneness. This "Oneness" means that all knowledge, and everything about us, is known, and we, the person inside who you call "I" or "Me" are made of the same

Conscious soul energy as those in the Spiritual Realm of Heaven.

So, what do our Guardian Angels s know of our personal future? Well, firstly they know our Life Plan and Life Challenges. Some of the Life Plan and challenges will have already happened and are now in the past. We may want a better future, and Angel messages will help identify the past events that have been difficult, and then help to identify our future, and change it towards a better course, giving us the potential for greater happiness and fulfilment.

Our Guardian Angels allow us to see some of the future that has already been planned, but not everything. In order to pick up what they are prepared to show us concerning our personal future we need to learn how to live our lives feeling and resonating more closely with them. This is extremely important in my teachings, and if we can follow it through this alone may change our lives in a positive way forever!

The vast intelligence in the Spiritual Realm of Heaven includes a knowingness of what everyone is doing. Imagine some huge computer program that combines events and stores the information of over seven billion people so that it can give the intelligent loving Source in Heaven, whom religions may call "God", a picture of the future.
The Source can also see events happing in nature, and to planet Earth. We may be given some of this picture, but only as they think we need, via our Guardian Angels. This view of the future will come as "Premonitions". The world will become a better and safer place if human beings could universally accept the existence of Heaven and our Guardian Angels, and then learn how to listen to them.

What spoils the plan, and what makes the world so blind? The answer is negative energy. The human beings who are totally self-centred, and totally lacking in empathy for other people, and for animals, nature, and the environment, are totally disconnected from their personal Guardian Angel. Guardian Angels resonate closely with us when we are caring and loving, and will not help us if we are self-centred.

Those in Heaven can see what people who are filled with negative, self-centred energy. Heaven can see what they are doing, and what they are likely to do. Those in Heaven cannot get through to such people because the main channel of communication is through our Guardian Angels.

Those in Heaven therefore get through to people who are resonating more closely with their Guardian Angels, in order to give them feelings, awareness, and a "Calling" to do what they can to work against the destruction caused by the self-centred ones.
If self-centred behaviour is at the heart of those in government of a nation, then everyone suffers. Alternatively, if those in government have policies of care towards others then many of the citizens of a nation will have more personal freedom, and a better quality of life.

CHAPTER EIGHT

THE MIRACLE OF CLAIRVOYANCE

The ability to see Angels and receive messages from them is a form of Clairvoyance. The term "Clairvoyance" means "All seeing". It is a gift that some people have been given. Although I do believe we all have some degree of clairvoyant ability. Some people try all types of spiritual development by studying religion, or through specific classes, or study healing methods and pagan rituals to acquire a greater clairvoyant gift. I do not recommend any of these. The word "gift" is important here. We are all given spiritual talents by God, and we have to visualise gifts as something that we can't acquire by ourselves. Instead we should focus on, and be proud, of the talents we have been given, and use them to give something back to the world.

Scientific instruments are designed to detect physical phenomena in our physical universe. The Conscious Energy of Heaven is the intelligent energy of a completely different dimension, and therefore our science of the physical world will never be able to fully detect or measure this energy in its attempts to find positive evidence of the existence of this other dimension.

I had given the lady, a complete stranger to me, whose son was in prison, and whose mother had passed, a reading using my clairvoyant gift. This is a miracle, and I am always very humbled by this because I know I am only a channel for what those on "The other side of life" wish to communicate.

So how can we detect this other dimension of Conscious Energy that we know as Heaven? Well, we ourselves are Conscious Energy. We are made of the same stuff. We have a link to this other dimension through our inner selves. It is through this link within us that we can in some small way sense the spiritual world. This is the only way that we will ever be able to see a place that science cannot detect.

The dimension of Conscious Energy (Heaven) is a very real place. It is a familiar place like going home. We were there before we were born. We return there after we leave our physical bodies at the end of physical life. It is a place of unconditional love all around. Love is the air we breathe in Heaven. I will go on to describe this place later in my accounts of some of the very vivid actual clairvoyant readings I have given. How can we prove all of this? Our scientific mindset, and our logical thoughts, are something I never try to argue about. Those who begin to believe are those who experience first-hand some personal life-changing phenomena concerning their own spirituality. When we are born our memories of where we came from are deliberately blanked out. So, I never try to argue with those who don't believe. They are only thinking and behaving in the way that they have been programmed at birth.

When I do a Clairvoyant Reading I see images, sometimes like still photos, and sometimes like a video film. The images are of those who have passed, stood close to the person I am reading, and of things they want to show me. This is usually where there is a bond of love or friendship. I always put a block on seeing images of anyone who wasn't a friend or loved one. I seem to know what they are saying by some kind of transfer of thoughts. I sometimes hear voices. I do not speak to the dead. I regard all those who make it safely across to this place which I will call "Heaven" as not being dead, but very much alive because the Highest Authority of all, whom we may name "God", has allowed them into Heaven.

Our soul is an energy made of the same energy as those in the Spiritual Realm. We are made of the same energy as the Angels. When trying to explain this I use the visual image of a car. When we see a car, then we may not see the driver inside. The windscreen can be reflective, leaving a view of the driver dark and unclear.
At the point of death of our physical body, to the real person inside it is just like getting out of a car. We stand outside of the car, and likewise stand outside of our physical body, look back and think "Was that me?" "I am still the same person".

Another way of looking at this is to imagine yourself as a baby. Many years later picture an image of yourself as an adult. Your body has changed beyond recognition, and yet you are still the same person inside.

Research into seeing the future

As a clairvoyant I am given visions by the Angels of some of the future. Some of the future for individuals. Some of the future on a local and global basis.

Starting in my teenage years I became frustrated at the lack of real knowledge about the meaning of life. My clairvoyant visions and premonitions were showing me a much bigger picture than society seemed to acknowledge.
Who or what are we? Just a human body or do we have a soul? Who is correct, science or religion?
Has life evolved, or was life and the physical universe created? If religion, then which religion is right? Religions themselves often criticise other religions as not being correct.
All these questions led me on a journey of spiritual research, so far lasting over 40 years.
Through clairvoyance I sense the Angel messages that enable me to do mediumship and psychic readings, and I have significantly expanded my knowledge about the meaning of life. I call this

"The System" for want of a better description.

The System

Our True inner self is a spiritual energy. Our soul cannot be seen by our physical eyes, nor can it be detected by scientific instruments.
There are many energies around us that we cannot see, touch, grasp, hear, smell. The most powerful of all these energies is gravity.
We cannot see radio waves, television signals, mobile phone signals, yet these are very real, and we accept them.
The person we are is our soul energy. Our soul is our personality that does not change when we pass across to Heaven.
When we are born, our memory of the Heaven is deliberately blanked. This is because we have to live our life with no memory of this beautiful place. We have a Life Plan to see through, and Life Lessons to experience, and hopefully learn from.
Many people are concerned about the future. Most of us have hopes and dreams.
For younger and middle-aged people, seeing and working towards a future as a time when life will be "Better", or achieving fulfilment of our dreams is important.
For people in the latter years of life the future can be a time of fear and uncertainty. Perhaps fear of death, and fear of old age, ill health and pain.
Clairvoyantly, working with our Guardian Angels, the future can be partially seen. The future can also be steered towards positive change. If a person tells me that they see or fear something bad about their future, I can sometimes ask the Angels to "Block" this from happening.
Limitations: In a brutally controlled society, or a brutally controlled relationship positive change can be difficult to achieve.

What can a clairvoyant see concerning the Future?

Fortune Tellers are psychics who have some ability to see the future if they are genuine. People might want to know what the future holds for their love lives, family relationships, health, wealth and career.

Mystics who see premonitions of the future have long been viewed as eccentric, yet often over time their predictions came true.

In my view it is a time, a new era, where clairvoyant visions, predictions and premonitions can be analysed logically, documented, and become an acceptable pseudo-science, understood more widely.

There are many ways of "Divination" such as seeing the future through Tarot Cards, Astrology, Palm Reading. I don't use any of these methods, and cannot comment on their accuracy. Our own Free Will is commonly understood to have led us to where we are today, and defines our actions and future Life Events. My research has surprisingly led to the conclusion that future events on our Life Plan will happen irrespective of our daily free will decisions.

Free will certainly influences our daily routine. Yet, we can sacrifice some of our free will to another person when in a close relationship with them. We can sacrifice some of our free will by caring for someone, and helping them in everyday tasks.

I am currently receiving premonitions concerning Climate Change, but equally as disturbing I am receiving premonitions of the latter part of the 21st century when fossil fuels are in serious short supply. In particular oil supply. It will be impossible to feed the world population, currently over 7 billion. The latter part of the 21st century will see the population shrink by half, and the human suffering of starvation and wars will be greater than planet earth has ever seen.

Other factors at play in reading our future include: Life Lessons

Clairvoyants all have their own ways of interpreting the spiritual energies and messages that may or may not refer to the future.

Personally, my clairvoyant ability to receive messages from the Angels gives me the following information:

1. A reasonably clear view of the future for a person up to two months ahead
2. Future events, people and happenings on a personal pre-ordained Life Plan
3. I might get a sudden psychic "Grounding" when giving someone a reading. This happens when I need to stop trying to see their future and instead evaluate their life up to now, and in the present. This is usually because self-destructive behaviour needs identifying, otherwise it will continue to have a major influence on that person's future.
4. I try to focus on the good, positive aspects of a person's future. I never give people bad news about the future.
5. What happens if I see something bad? I can block it – stop the bad thing from happening.

I can warn people if the bad thing is some natural disaster. I have warned people over the years not to travel to certain areas of the world. Subsequently they didn't travel to these places which did really suffer natural disasters. These warnings included a premonition of a tsunami, and a severe weather event in the Philippines. Future Global and regional events seem to be easier to see if I am clairvoyantly reading someone who is to travel a different part of the world or travel anywhere.

CHAPTER NINE

Discovering the Meaning of Life

Introduction
Most human beings have their own spiritual beliefs.
My personal clairvoyant abilities came to me inadvertently through a vision following many years of research i ithas stood the test of time for me and have proven essential to my on-going understanding of the spiritual visions and messages that I receive.
For those who are open minded concerning this "System", I feel that this knowledge may help people begin to understand the true "Bigger Picture" and start to "Open-up" to sensing their Guardian Angels.

For me personally, understanding the System is an absolute in my interpreting the messages and visions that I experience. The Spiritual System has been the subject of my research for more than 40 years. Sometimes the visions are powerful, sometimes faint. The energies that I perceive can overwhelm the senses or be faint energies at the extreme periphery of perception. By understanding the System, and knowing what these energies are, and their meaning and significance, the information they bring can be interpreted, and made sense of correctly.

The System Outline

There are two main universes: the physical universe, and the spiritual universe. Their energies balance each other.
The spiritual universe has its own laws of physics that cannot be

detected by the science of our physical universe.

The spiritual universe is an almost infinite, vast energy, and is a conscious intelligence. I call it the dimension of "Conscious Energy".

Our soul, the person we call "I" or "Me", is made of conscious energy. Our true home is the spiritual universe.

There is a vast intelligence at the centre of the spiritual universe, a source of all creation and purpose. We are born out of this "Source" (whom religions may name "God").

When we are in the spiritual universe the energy that we feel, almost like air that we breathe, is that of unconditional love.

We will live through many lives over thousands of years. The purpose of each life is for adventure, experience, and to spiritually grow more caring and loving of other souls, and Creation. We eventually end up merging back into the Source.

There are many spiritual beings in the spiritual universe. I name them "Angels". They have many different roles. Their purpose is to help care for us, and for nature, and for the planet.

We each have at least one Angel dedicated to helping us. We can describe such Angels as "Guardian Angels" or "Angel Guides".

After each life we have a period of spiritual rest, and a life review. We may stop for many years (although there is no time in the spiritual universe) and look over those still in life whom we love. At some point it will be necessary to move on within the spiritual realm, probably in readiness for being born again into a new life.

Before each life, we are given a "Life Plan". A Life Plan will include things we will do in life, people we will meet, plus much more. We are also set "Life Challenges". Such challenges will be difficult, but we will learn much from the experiences, and hopefully become a better person.

After we are born, our memory of the Spiritual Realm is forgotten, and our Life Plan, and Life Challenges are not held in our conscious mind. However, our Angel Guides know these plans and challenges, and will try to help us throughout life. The secret is learning to be closer to our Angel Guides so that we can feel the help they try to give us.

Our Angel Guides try to help people in the following ways:
They are a link between ourselves, and our loved-ones in Heaven
They are a channel for healing
They know our life situation, and will try to help and guide us
They know some of our future, and will allow us to see some of our future
They may bring us premonitions concerning the future.

Who, and What are we?

Our True inner self is a spiritual energy. Our soul cannot be seen by our physical eyes, nor can it be detected by scientific instruments.
There are many energies around us that we cannot see, touch, grasp, hear, smell. The most powerful of all these energies is gravity.
We cannot see radio waves, television signals, mobile phone signals, yet these are very real, and we accept them.
The person we are is our soul energy. Our soul is our personality that does not change when we pass across to Heaven.
When we are born, our memory of the spiritual realm is deliberately blanked. This is because we have to live our life with no memory of this beautiful place. We have a Life Plan to see through, and Life Lessons to experience, and hopefully learn from.

My early spiritual experiences

A ten-month old baby struggling for life with severe life-threatening asthma could be observed lying in a cot in an oxygen tent. The location was a hospital in the city of Bradford, Yorkshire, England. The year was 1951.

The baby was me, and up to the age of 10 months I had been a healthy baby, but having been given a childhood vaccine the day before, I now had suffered an immune system reaction, and started with severe asthma that could not be brought under control.

The police officer knocked loudly on the front door of a Victorian terrace house in the city of Bradford, Yorkshire, England, and the city was enveloped by a heavy fog of mist and smoke from the industry powered by coal, coal fires warming the houses, and the local chimneys of cotton mills and woollen mills . The locals gave a name for this pollution as "Smog".

It was late evening and a young couple apprehensively opened the door to a male police officer who said, "We have just received a call from the hospital. Your baby son is near death and won't survive the night". Very few people had a home telephone in 1951. Telephones were a luxury of the wealthy, very few people owned a car, and in the years soon after World War Two most people didn't have many of the things that we take for granted in the 21st century.

The young couple were my parents, and I was the baby. I had been a fit and healthy baby, but a diphtheria vaccination triggered severe asthma which hospitalised me, leaving me struggling for life lying in a cot in an oxygen tent.

My parents were only allowed to visit once weekly, and then only to observe me through a glass window to help prevent infection. This appeared to be the procedure throughout my time in hospital – over eighteen months. The police called at my parents' home on several occasions throughout that period because I was near to death.

My parents caught the first bus available next morning to the hospital, feeling distraught, only to find with joy and much emotion that I had made a significant recovery and was no longer in danger.

This was the first time that I had been close to death, but I continued to have recurrent severe asthma attacks with all the crisis that an asthma attack brings.

Do infants remember their lives at such a young age? My detailed memory of all this is not there, but I do clearly remember times when I was no longer in my body but in a warm secure loving place with a loving spiritual being. My speech as an infant wasn't fully developed but the feelings were that I was rescued from my suffering body and had spent a lot of time with this beautiful being. I was then sent back to my body and immediately experienced the suffering again. I remember feeling "I don't want to go back", only to be told "You have to go back".

Looking back on this time now, I realise that the beautiful loving being is my Guardian Angel. We all have a Guardian Angel, and in this book I will explain how these beautiful beings stay with us and try to help us throughout our lives and beyond this life.

What were my memories of this time? I remember being with a loving Angel figure, no wings, just a beautiful loving being who cared for me. Most of the time I felt no suffering, but existed in a secure place, surrounded by love. I knew I was somewhere else, not in the body of that suffering infant. I didn't want to go back into my body, but somehow, I had to. There was no language in communicating this to me, just feelings, just a "Knowingness".

I was left with permanent asthma. I would get frequent attacks, and symptoms became acute with exercise, so I could never participate in sport. I missed half of my school life and was always a sickly child. However, like many people with a disability, I eventually became more determined to succeed than most, and achieved high grades in school, before leaving in my mid-teens to pursue a career in accountancy.

Throughout my childhood the experience of being with my Guardian Angel, and still feeling my Guardian Angel with me was constant. I failed to understand violence. Why do some children start fights and cause hurt? Why does it give some children pleasure to bully others? Why do children cause psychological hurt to others by calling them names? Why do children and adults cause pain to others – isn't there enough pain in daily survival?

Of course, I understand now that much of this behaviour is a part of growing up, but such behaviour for many, many people is still there in adulthood. We live in a world that is advanced in science but suffers much spiritually primitive behaviour caused by many adults. Often those in positions of power and authority have attained their positions by walking over others. Alternatively, authority and leadership can, of course, be attributed to "Survival of the fittest". This would imply that spiritual forces at work might intend that to happen.

However, throughout my childhood, into adult life, and still to this day I realise two things:

1) Sometimes we cannot help hurting others – life throws situations at us on a daily basis. How we react and respond can never be perfect.

2) Should we deliberately hurt others, if we are too self-centred and have very little empathy for others, then this causes hurt

and is spiritually wrong.

My awareness of Guardian Angels opened a door to my spiritual awareness. There is a clairvoyant gift in my family, and visions, premonitions and my enhanced intuitive feelings became a normal part of my life.

However, living in a modern world of science, materialism, and new technological advances, I found conflict with my spiritual experiences. My logical mind had to find proof of my spirituality. I am an accountant, I have a car, computers, and immerse myself fully in the world around.

Of course, I was born into a world where science rules. Historically science and religion have been at total odds with each other. I use the word "Religion" because almost all spiritual beliefs are classified as either "Religious beliefs and experiences" being good, and every other spiritual experience as being bad.

THE ARCHANGEL

On a beautiful Spring morning, 1st May 1999 I awoke at 6am to find sunshine penetrating the curtains.

As I lay resting in bed, realising this was a Saturday morning and thinking that I don't have to get up for work, something wonderful happened. A spiritual face appeared in front of me. The face was that of an Archangel. I felt fearful, but then a reassuring feeling came across from this incredible Being who was radiating golden light. His face was itself a golden light. The eyes were what drew my attention. A feeling that He knew everything about me, but understood, and that He forgave my mistakes and imperfections. His love was, and is, unconditional.

This book isn't about religion. I am a Christian, having been baptised in the Church of England as a baby and then baptised again with a fundamental Church in Keighley, Yorkshire at the age of 19 years. For most of my life I hadn't attended Church, but still tried to live a Christian lifestyle. Although I knew I had some "Sixth Sense", I had always been very sceptical of clairvoyants, mediums, psychics, and fortune tellers. Firstly, Christians don't approve of what they do. Secondly my logical mind simply thought of them as nonsense. This same logical mind had spent a lifetime trying to find the meaning of life. Although by profession I am an accountant, I had made an amateur study of astronomy, astrophysics, and quantum physics. I subscribed to the magazine "New Scientist", avidly devouring the latest scientific discoveries and theories. I had studied religious beliefs. I loved nature. Dogs, cats, horses, rabbits, birds, all animals to me seemed to have someone inside looking out. It isn't just human beings who have a soul. The trees, flowers, plants, and all of nature, seem to vibrate with a life-giving energy from a divine source. Equally importantly I had also listened to people. I listened to real life experiences. So many ordinary people over the years would recount their own real-life experiences of ghosts. On every occasion I was always very willing to listen because to me there was a need to evaluate the situation. Old ladies would tell me how they knew their deceased husband was still close by. All of these things are spiritual experiences that Christians have to deny. All of these things are largely ignored by many people in modern, scientific, materialistic societies. They think about education, career, work, family, things to buy, holidays, sport. All these are good, normal things. All are a part of life. Then when someone they know and love passes from life they are thrown into a desolate place of grief and loss, with no answers from anyone.

What is it all about?
So now, here I am, lying in bed with the face of a Heavenly Being, an Archangel, in front of me. I heard no words but just knew instantly what I was being told. I suddenly felt myself rising-up at great speed to enter a new dimension and saw before me a beautiful place. "This is First Heaven" was the knowledge implanted in my thoughts. What I saw before me I will now describe.
Firstly, I will describe the feelings. At first, I sensed a pleasant

caressing feeling of gentle warmth. This grew quickly into a feeling of love. Yes, I could FEEL love as something tangible. I realised that love was all around just like the air we breathe. I felt at ease in this relaxed atmosphere of love. I began to understand this was what some people describe as "Unconditional Love". I felt important and loved even though I knew I was far from perfect.

This new dimension is very real. I could see a rock-solid landscape of a green valley before my eyes. It struck me how vivid the colours hit my vision everywhere I turned, with vivid shades of green grass, the leaves of trees, and every shade of flower vibrating in the beauty and aura of an eternal Spring morning. The colours of the flowers were of yellow, red, purple, white, and each flower seemed to glow with an aura of life energy. A gentle breeze seemed to move the grass, the trees, and the flowers. I could see real people, not grey, transparent ghosts, but real people wearing normal clothing! Their clothing was in normal colours. Real animals were moving around just ignoring me because they had no fear, because there is no fear in Heaven. Some were wild animals. Others were pets, mainly dogs, cats, and one or two horses, and obviously were there to accompany some of the people I could see. The most noticeable feeling within the feeling of love was of the profound beauty of this new "World", this other dimension that is more real than the physical earth we live on. I felt a familiarity as if I had arrived back home after an adventure into the earth plane. I didn't think to look at myself, my hands or feet, but felt my personality as my normal self, but with a profound sense of well-being, and a floating feeling with no discomfort, no pain. People were walking around yet I felt they could simply move to some other place if they wanted, through their thoughts.

I could see houses like on earth, as if they were there to give a feeling of being at home to those who had passed. I could also see in the distance beautiful white buildings. I was stood in this lush green valley, and the nearest building was a thatched farmhouse. A man and his wife emerged from the farmhouse to look at me. I got the feeling that this was the same type of house they had lived in whilst in the physical world. Elsewhere in the valley people were busy, but at a steady pace. Some were gardening, tending to the flowers. I asked the Heavenly Being who was still with me where was everyone else? There should surely be many millions of people in Heaven. I could only see perhaps 30 or 40 people. The answer came instantly with a clear vision in my thoughts of many people simply resting in the white buildings in the distance. Also, that there are many valleys, and many, many different places in this very real dimension. I didn't know at the time that I would come to see many of these other places in my future role as a clairvoyant.

I noticed the sky was a hazy blue, yet an all-pervading brightness and energy emanated from above. I wondered if above the place I was visiting there was a Higher place. My thoughts were instantly read! "Come, I will show you this Higher place," said this Heavenly Being. I then found myself flying upwards at speed into the sky through a barrier of white, almost like cloud, to emerge into another level of Heaven, which I now call "Second Heaven". This dimension is incredibly bright. This dimension wasn't a solid real world like the lower dimension of Heaven. It was as if I was floating in a brilliant white mist with no sign of ground or sky or distance. White radiant Beings were busy working. They could be described as Angels without wings. I knew what they were doing. They were organising everything, keeping both the dimension of Heaven, and the physical dimension supported. Above them I saw a sky of brilliant white light and felt an overwhelming and infinite energy of warmth and unconditional love. This energy was a vast loving intelligence, yet with the oneness of a person. A person who is neither a "He" nor a "She". This was the infinitely divine person who is the source of all knowledge, intelligence, meaning and purpose. I realised that this Divine Consciousness of He/ She is the Oneness, connected to the "Me" or "I" inside each one of us. This Light above me was the Source, the Creator, the centre of purity and of love and purpose. This Light above me was God. I call the

Highest Heaven "Third Heaven".

I looked and received smiles of love from some of the Angelic Beings nearby. They were very busy working, looking after life, and very intent in their purpose.

The Heavenly Being who accompanied me was Spiritually Higher than the Angels for I knew that they were looking at Him with respect as a part of the Highest spiritual authority, a part of God. There was a feeling of the Heavenly Being having much, much more work to do, and that it was time for me to go. I didn't realise that from now on in my work on Earth I would catch glimpses of this place many times again. The Heavenly Being concluded the visit with a message:

"I will now leave you and I grant you the full spiritual gift of CLAIRVOYANCE to see the Angels and see through to First Heaven. I also pass to you the gift of spiritual discernment, to have the wisdom to discern between good and evil spirits.

Your work will be to help others with these spiritual gifts, for the world is in much need of spiritual understanding and direction".

I immediately found myself back in bed again. The time had moved from 6am to 6.30am. That half hour changed my life forever.

What happens when we pass across to the "Other Side of Life"? The following account is fictional but incorporates most of the experiences that we can go through.

John

John struggled for breath as he ran uphill. Sweat was pouring down his face, and he was beginning to feel exhausted. He was angry. His girlfriend, and partner of seven years, had just finished their relationship and gone off with some skinny, balding solicitor. John was nicely built and worked as a joiner but knew that his ex-partner always put money before everything else in her endless shopping sprees. Her new boyfriend was not short of money and that's what she went for.
These thoughts and feelings going around his head made him even more determined to continue running.
It was a hot June day and John was doing a half marathon to help raise money for cancer.
His father had died of a sudden heart attack when John was only 12 years old, leaving his mother to finish bringing him up. Cruel cancer had recently taken the life of his mother just six months earlier. This made it even harder to bear the loss of his girlfriend as well, but true to John's caring nature he was determined to complete the half marathon and raise some money towards supporting cancer research.
The half marathon was well organised, and at age 36 John appeared to be one of the participants in the race who should be

able to complete it with relative ease.

He took a brief stop to take on some water. He drank a couple of mouthfuls then poured the remaining water over himself in a cool refreshing moment, as a waterfall of clear spring water. Then he was on his way again.

John was feeling breathless and sharp pains kept piercing his chest. His only thoughts were that he was out of condition and would book some time down at the gym starting next week.

Still, he pushed on.

Suddenly his chest was gripped, as if in a vice. He fell to the floor. He could see the ground in front of him and hear the voices of people rushing to his aid. He couldn't move.

Then all went black.

First aiders tried to resuscitate him. Paramedics arrived. The race organisers had everything in place for those who might need medical help. Rushing to John's aid were people with medical expertise. Within a couple of minutes the blue lights of an ambulance. He was pronounced dead on arrival at hospital.

John wouldn't have known but the rare heart condition that had taken the life of his father at a young age was genetic and had now claimed a second victim.

All was black. John suddenly found himself awake. He was looking down on a scene of commotion below. An ambulance, and people milling around someone laid out on the ground. He felt free, not just free of the heaviness of a body struggling in a marathon, not just free of the pain across his chest, but free of the anger, free of the emotions that had taken over his life in recent months.

A beautiful light appeared, and he felt himself being pulled towards the light by some invisible force. Yet, he didn't feel afraid. He knew that his spirit was free and somehow all the cares and worries of his everyday life disappeared. He realised that he had died but for some reason wasn't bothered. He didn't want to go back into life. As John fell into the light a vortex in the shape of a tunnel emerged and he was drawn at high speed towards the tunnel. He found himself moving through this swirling vortex at high speed with a sense of anticipation, and a profound feeling of love surrounding him. He felt the love surrounding and protecting him as he began to perceive another light which gradually became brighter and brighter. It was the most beautiful light he had ever seen and he felt totally at ease. There now appeared two shapes at the end of the tunnel. The shapes became clearer, and he realised that these were two people who were waiting to meet him.

John emerged suddenly from the vortex of the tunnel into a beautiful garden. He immediately recognised the two people.
"Mum…Dad, you're here to meet me!"
"We love you, so much, son" said his father. Mum smiled and gave him a hug. An embrace, that became two souls merging together, through the binding love of mother and son.
"You pushed yourself too hard," his mum commented. "We were watching over you. You should have got yourself checked out for any heart problems knowing how your father passed".

John was still trying to familiarise himself with his new surroundings. It somehow didn't matter to him that his life was over. He remembered an old saying "Life is but a moment". This place he was in now was so beautiful. He felt alive, and the air he breathed was an atmosphere of love beyond description.

Mum explained that she and dad had a home here – just like the family home back in the physical world. Then his thoughts made him laugh as he said to his Dad: "This place is more real than the world we lived in". Beyond the garden he could now see the family home, and in the distance were beautiful mountains. He could see the landscape of a green valley, and nearby flowers danced in a delicate breeze as their colours radiated in vivid splendour far more intense than on earth. What surprised him was that everything was real, solid, with vibrant colours. Heaven isn't a misty, intangible place. Animals are across there in Heaven, but they have no fear and simply ignored the human souls and continued grazing in the lush grass. People who cared for pets such as dogs, cats, and horses appeared to have these much-loved animals with them. The love bond between a person and that of their devoted pet shone out as a connection that spans the dimensions of earth and heaven.

John realised that Heaven was a familiar place. He had been here before. It was like coming home.

"What happens next, Mum?" was John's question after what seemed like an eternity in simply taking-in the beauty of his surroundings.

His mum replied "Well, in your case we've been told there won't be much rest. Many souls like your dad and I can spend as long as we wish just resting. However, your Guardian has told us that they have an urgent mission for you. This mission will be shared by many souls who are like you".

"Guardian? Do you mean Guardian Angel?" said John.

Mum replied, "Well, those souls who are more advanced can be called Guardian Angels or Spirit Guides. They try to look after us, but many people live reckless lives of their own free will. However, your Guardian will be here soon. Dad and I don't know what this mission is all about. They say it is "Most unusual".

Sleep fell upon John. He awoke to see a beautiful woman stood next to him. "Julia, Julia, is that you?"

A woman who appeared to be in her early thirties, dark flowing hair, and a flowing silver dress that shimmered like stars. Her smile was captivating. Her eyes showed a depth of love and compassion that reflected an eternal bond.

"John, I have been waiting for you for many years"

"You are, or should I say you were my wife" said John. "Oh, my beautiful Julia. I never thought I would see you again!"

John then began to feel disorientated. "I didn't have a wife, I was single. My girlfriend had just split up with me".

"Come with me," said Julia. "Those who have recently left the physical realm often feel confused. You need a time of peace and adjustment. Come, take my hand".

John joined hands with Julia and felt himself lifted up as if he weighed nothing, and was flying over beautiful valleys, houses, and a landscape so beautiful beyond any imagination. Eventually they came to rest along the shore of a lake. Contrasting shades of light shimmered in the lake before them. The movement created patterns that appeared to be alive in dancing with the joy and beauty of this place. Feelings of peace and love were overwhelming.

"I was your wife in your previous life," said Julia. "We were married for over 40 years. You died in 1970. I lived on until 1983. After I passed across to Heaven, I didn't want another life. You are my soulmate and I just wanted to wait here for you. You always were a determined soul and volunteered for another life to be born in 1989, even though you were warned that it would only be a short life because of the genetic heart defect from your earth parents."

"How come you know me as John?"

Julia laughed. "You were named John as my husband. When you were born into a new life in 1989, I whispered in the ear of your earth parents to name you John, and fortunately they seemed to feel that was the name to give you. You will learn that those in spirit such as ourselves can whisper in the ear of those in the physical realm, but they don't always listen!" Julia laughed. "You never listened. I couldn't get through to you no matter how hard I tried!"

An eternity of peace, love, companionship of soulmates now seemed to pass as the two sat beside this lake of beauty and tranquillity. Time does not exist in the reality of Heaven. The only time is that of "The Now", "The Moment", "The Instant". Without the clutter of thoughts and worries about yesterday or tomorrow the time of "Now" becomes incredibly intense. John thought to himself. How he wished he had realised the value of appreciating every moment, every second of his physical life on earth. What a lesson that would have been in reducing his stress and worries, and of intensifying his everyday experience. Julia suddenly spoke: "I agree". John laughed realising that they were as one and their thoughts and feelings were shared.

John fell asleep. Julia woke him to ask if he felt ready to move on. "We will soon have a meeting to attend," said Julia. "First, you must go to the Library for your life review."

John remembered the Library from his previous lives. A brilliant white building filled with books. John had lived in the digital age when books were becoming less in printed version, and everything available online. Yet the Library still looked like shelves filled with printed books.

Another soul appeared and stood alongside John. "I am your Angel Guide," said the radiant soul who had the appearance of a kind but strict elderly teacher. "My name is Matthew, and it is time to review the life you have just been through."

John could see a book with his name on it.

Matthew said, "You lived a good life as a very caring person. You did make one or two mistakes. Turn to page 23, and you'll see a date of May 31st 2010".

John opened the page. As he opened the page it became alive like a video, and then suddenly he was pulled into the scene. It was May 31st 2010 and he had received a phone call to say his closest friend Gary was in hospital. John had been too busy with his own problems to visit him and had not fully realised how Gary had missed his friend in his time of need.

Matthew said, "You can't put things right, John. You can see and feel how hurt Gary was because you ignored his needs."

John realised that he was being taught a lesson. Life on earth is like a school. We are all there for the experiences that life throws at us, and to learn to be as caring and loving of others around us as possible even in the hardest of times.

"Don't worry," said Matthew. "You are quite an advanced soul. There were not many times in your life when you didn't show care and love for others. You can imagine how many souls find this a very harrowing time as they review lives that in some

cases showed disregard and lack of love and care for people around. Where they caused deliberate hurt then they are made to feel the pain they caused, be it emotional or physical pain. Your life review has been easy, and over much more quickly than that of many others!"
As John left the Library with Matthew, Julia joined them. The Light of the Source shone above. A light that is brighter than any light in the physical universe yet does not dazzle. The energy from the Light is of pure unconditional love. John couldn't help but feel that he was a part of, and connected to everything, and that the entire spiritual universe was joined together as just one infinitely vast oneness. John suddenly knew that all human beings, and all animals have a soul energy connected to the "Oneness". John realised that the spiritual life energies that look after trees, plants, flowers, insects, and the Earth, are all connected with the "Oneness". John knew instantly that to hurt any part of the "Oneness" was like hurting oneself.

John slept again. Sleep in the dimension of Heaven seemed to be a natural part of the sequence between contemplation, activity, learning, and experiencing the sheer beauty and joy of this place. He could hear the sound of music.

CHAPTER TEN

First Heaven

In unity with many religions, the clairvoyant experience is one of perceiving "Heaven" as a place from which unconditional love emanates. There is definitely a "Oneness" of all soul energy culminating in the ultimate Source that I still call "God" from my Christian upbringing, and the many years spent in my adult life as an active Christian. However, the real images I see as a clairvoyant "Seeing through to Heaven" differ from most descriptions of Heaven by religious teachings.

What Does Heaven Look Like?

I name the first place we go to when we pass away from physical life "First Heaven".
It can be seen clairvoyantly as a very real, solid dimension, more real, and as a more intense experience than our physical world.

There are gardens, beautiful valleys, trees, grass, flowers. Colours are intense, vivid, and seemingly radiating energy. Animals may appear as animals with no fear, and no aggression. People can still appear as people, although we mainly appear in our soul state as what we are – intelligent conscious energy.

First Heaven is the only place in Heaven that can be perceived clairvoyantly. Heaven has many other places. If you look up at the night sky and try to imagine the vastness of the physical universe with billions of stars in every galaxy and seemingly endless numbers of galaxies then that is also how big Heaven is. My research has given me theories concerning the other Heavens. There is a place in Heaven where we move on to after out time in First Heaven which seems to be our true spiritual home. In this spiritual home we may re-unite with our eternal soulmates who are our true friends.

There are other places in Heaven where we move to prepare ourselves for another life as a human being. Heaven is a place of Creation and has places where plants, flowers and the diversity of life can be created.

There are of course higher Heavens as souls progress through many lives towards unity with the ultimate Source, closer to God.

Having given many thousands of readings, almost everyone I helped found that the reading provided evidence of survival of the soul of a loved one beyond physical death.

I am invariably overwhelmed by the beauty of the experience and the positive benefit to the person whom I a reading. For me, every reading seems like a miracle, as it does to the majority of people whom I help. Modern day miracles really can happen. Only afterwards would my enquiring mind think through what had happened. My first thought was usually: "What have I learnt about Heaven from the reading?"

The truth is that I have learnt a little more aout First Heaven and that has to be sufficient for our learning capbility whilst in life as human beings.

Every reading I have given is as different as each of the people I helped. The readings also showed me evidence of Heaven from different perspectives, for every person has their own spiritual way of relating to Heaven.

I can understand the religious descriptions of Heaven as being "Holy" with teachings of spiritual love.

The unconditional LOVE in Heaven really is an energy, and that energy is something we need to feel as a part of our natural soul state. We can experience and be a part of that LOVE without religious beliefs.

I can look at Heaven in a mystical way, yet also in a matter-of-fact way, as another dimension that must have its own laws of physics. Above all else the spiritual dimension of Heaven is a place of infinite intelligence. It is the place of what I call "Conscious Energy". Our soul, the real "I" or "Me" inside all of us is made of the same Conscious Energy. Heaven is our familiar, friendly, true home from where we came before birth, and where we return after our physical life as a human being comes to an end.

When I describe First Heaven I have to clarify that it is not the vision of Heaven as I imagined it from a Christian perspective. Throughout the later years in my life I have been able to see through to First Heaven because I let go of the limitations of religious belief. I come from an active Christian background. I trained as a Methodist preacher and led over 100 Church Sunday Services throughout a four-year period. My family has members who belong to the Catholic and the Anglican faiths which led me to attend services at most of the major Christian denominations.

I receive messages via the Angels from those who are in First Heaven and this might be looked-on as speaking to the dead. Holy Scripture teaches that it is a sin to "Speak to the dead" which is why many people think that mediums and clairvoyants are wrong in what they do. Back in the year 2004, my final year as a preacher, my clairvoyant gift became stronger. I had to reconcile my thoughts because I was suppressing my clairvoyant gift due to religious beliefs. I had to find the strength to go with my heart. I realised that nothing I could say would avoid condemnation from those who hold strong Christian beliefs. I therefore needed to assess the situation just for myself so that I could find the determination to dedicate myself to neutral, non-religious spiritual research. I knew that Heaven wanted me to help people with my clairvoyant gift without inner fears of committing sin. Heaven was giving me the visions and messages via the Angels.

The conclusions I reached confirmed that I was not committing sin. I was not speaking to the dead. My communication with Heaven is simply to receive visions and messages from the Angels.

Whenever I do a reading, I realise that I cannot speak with those who have passed. The Guardian Angels from Heaven give me a vision of the person in spirit, and it is the Angels that give me messages from the deceased soul. Sometimes the person I am giving a reading seeks to ask questions. I have to tell them that I find that I cannot ask questions because they will not be answered. Yet, surprisingly the deceased soul, communicating through the Angels would invariably give me messages for the person that were the most important ones. It was as if Heaven knew the questions that were burning inside of the heart of the person I was reading.

So, I am not speaking with the so called "Dead". Another point that helps me to justify any internal conflict with my Christian faith is that "Dead" usually refers to people who are dead to sin. Those souls that have been allowed into Heaven, by the Grace of God are not dead to sin, but very much alive in their soul state. The big surprise to myself as I progressed through many thousands of readings to help people who are mostly non-religious, is that most people make it through to Heaven even if their life was less than perfect.

In First Heaven we will all experience a "Life Review" where we are made to see the hurt that we have caused others. It is only truly evil people who do not make it to Heaven, usually by their own choice, because they realise that their life review will not be easy. Such evil and tormented souls sometimes choose to stay Earthbound for a while, often manifesting as ghosts. Eventually all these souls are gathered up to be dealt with by Heaven, but not before they may have caused some fear and upset as evil earthbound energies.

The overwhelming majority of souls do make it safely to First Heaven, yet once in Heaven their ability to communicate seems almost impossible other than through clairvoyance. I believe that Heaven respects the right of those in life to live without interference from spirits.

First Heaven is a transient place where our soul is allowed to rest after the end of physical life. One of my first discoveries, which came as a huge surprise to me, is that the first place many of us will reach is a place that may be similar to our home in life, and similar to the world around that we knew in life. This is to help us transition and not feel unease at what has happened in the process of so called "Death" where, in reality, we find ourselves still able to see and hear. We still have feelings, and we can still think. We realise that we are still the same person with our memories intact, although worries and stress are no longer there. I will explain the reason for this later.

The following is a true account concerning the parents of a lady I was reading.

Anne came to see me. I picked up that her adult daughter was having a difficult time with life. This proved to be the case because her daughter's husband had recently died, suspected suicide. What came through on the reading was a message from this husband saying it was an unintentional combination of his medical condition, diabetes, and alcohol abuse that had caused his death. The following week Anne came back to see me with her daughter. The messages from the deceased husband helped ease the pain, and then a message came through from Anne's mother. I firstly gave Anne a description of her mother. With my clairvoyant ability, I see a vision of the deceased person, often in great detail. As usual I gave a full description including that of hairstyle, hair colour, height and build and clothing. I was then given a vision of Anne's mother and father living in a cottage in Wales with beautiful mountain scenery nearby. This seemed strange because Anne had an obvious Yorkshire accent, and we were located in East Yorkshire. Anne, however, was amazed at the description of the home in Wales. She told me that she was Welsh, and her parents had lived in the family home in Wales, as described by me, until the death of her father. Anne's mother had spent the final years of her life living with Anne In Yorkshire.

Amidst all the emotions of Anne and her daughter there was a healing process. It was only afterwards that I thought about her mother and father still together in a home that resembled their family home in Wales. The house was real, yet I knew that they were in Heaven. They were not ghosts haunting the real physical home in Wales. Heaven had given them the familiar home surroundings to be together for as long as they needed as they transition from their needs as human beings carried with them from their Earthly lives. I often find that loving parents remain in this transition place for another reason, and that is so that can still look over the lives of children or other loved ones still in physical life. We don't stay in these surroundings forever, but certainly as long as we wish, perhaps until our loved ones on Earth have eventually passed-on from their lives as human beings.

My logical, spiritual research indicates that there are energies that connect the dimension of the physical universe and the spiritual dimension of Heaven. These energies cross back and forth between dimensions and can replicate physical landscapes and houses on Earth. I have seen this many times whilst receiving visions. I am suspicious that some of the energies theorised in quantum physics such as dark energy and dark matter might be inter-dimensional energies of enormous proportions. Physicists have been unable to identify these energies but know they exist. Perhaps it takes *something beyond* physical science to identify non-physical energies inter-acting with the physical universe.

A lady called Margaret came to see me for a reading. As usual, I asked her to tell me nothing, other than confirm or deny the visions and messages that the Angels gave me.

"I see your mother who must be in spirit". Margaret replied "Yes"". I then went in to give a description of her appearance and how she had died. Margaret then asked me "Where is my mother now?". I can't ask questions, but the vision suddenly changed to an image of her deceased mother sat in a comfortable chair in her lounge, knitting and watching television. "That's exactly how my mother would spend the happy, restful times", said Margaret. I then went on to describe the lounge in more detail. I could see an unusual light fitting, a chandelier. Margaret was astonished. "No-one could know that" she said.

Again, this reading and the visions held a different slant for me as a spiritual researcher. Heaven is real and when I say that I mean a very real, solid-looking dimension. I can conclude that the mirror image of energies from the physical world can be made to produce the same familiar surroundings and objects that were around us whilst in physical life. Also, that the spiritual universe is one of unimaginable intelligence and creative ability.

I then went on to relay a vision that the Angels gave me from Margaret's father. I gave a brief description of him, and how he had died of a heart attack, which Margaret confirmed as correct. I then received a further vision of him happily working under the bonnet of a red car which he seemed quite proud of. It had the appearance of a high-powered performance vehicle. The message accompanying the vision was that I was seeing what was doing in real time. Margaret was again astonished at such a clear vision and the mention of the car. "He spent all of his spare time working on cars as a hobby. The red car was his favourite!"

First Heaven

I see light everywhere
Gentle warmth of unconditional love
I am drawn into First Heaven, somehow
Just here, not above

I am free from life on Earth
From pain, suffering, happiness, pleasure
Back to my true home, somehow familiar
I cannot measure
………. The overwhelming love

Yes! I can still think and see, still same old me,
I see my loved ones who passed before,

waiting here for me
I see their faces, young again,
Together we fly free
Across beautiful valleys, green grass, trees, flowers
A very real Heaven created by the One with powers
..................of Creation

In the afterlife of Heaven we will at some point have a Life Review, accompanied by our Guardian Angel. Those who have hurt others are shown and made to feel the hurt they caused. This is a true form of Justice for those who thought they had "Got Away" with bad deeds by not being punished whilst alive as a human being. We are also shown the good things that we did. Loving and helping others, nature and the environment helps our growth and advancement as a spiritual being. Some people experience a "Life Review" before a meeting of "Wise Beings". Others may experience their Life Review in what can only be described as a "Library" in Heaven.

A Library in Heaven

My soul set free from my body, my life
I float on a path towards a building white,
The Heaven I hoped for shines all around
I breathe air of love, see beauty profound.

Heaven is light, love, joy and peace
Beauty, safety, I feel wonderful, at ease
I see radiant Angels, sense power
of the Creator above
Overwhelming, infinite, unconditional love.

Heaven offers rest, to recover from life's pain
Then time to review, start learning again.

A brilliant white building in front of me
Is a place of further learning, a Library

I see before me many books of life
For everyone who ever lived
their toils, their strife,
Their joy, sorrow, happiness, fun,
The times they had to fight, battles lost and won.

I see a book now, with my name bold and clear
Should I reach to grasp it?
My Angel guide says "Don't fear"
Each page is a day of your life we did give
Every moment, every minute
I may view and relive.

I open a page of happiness and joy
Go back to my childhood when I was a boy,
My Angel guide told me, in a most gentle way
to visit a page where my life went astray.
Did I hurt others?
I was blind but now see
I now feel the hurt, caused directly by me.

I can enter the page, and I'm in life again
At that moment in time when I caused someone pain
I can work it through differently
Not self-centred, but care,
Understand how others feel,
Learn how to share.

I awoke, it was dawn,
Was this a vision, had I dreamed?
I'm alive, not passed away
To the afterlife that seemed so real.

Visions of the Future

Visions of the Future can be given to us by those in First Heaven. Such visions can be faint and fleeting, but with an understanding of how Heaven tries to help us the visions are not lost.

When I see the future, I see visions of some things that will happen, and visions of some things that may or may not happen. If I see something bad, I try to "Block" it from happening, or make it somehow easier to deal with. I try to encourage good positive futures by using my own energies in that purpose.

Tunnel Vision

Deep-seated personal feelings within many of us about what we want to achieve, who we want to be, and the type of persons we want to be close to in our future.

These feelings were acquired by our soul in Heaven before we were born. Those with Tunnel Vision succeed when others who don't keep hold of that focus don't succeed.

The following is a story of three brothers. As in most families the brothers all had different characters. It would seem that each had a different inner spiritual awareness, although they would not think of it that way.

The eldest brother, John, didn't know which career to follow. His parents advised him to study for a career in accountancy because he had a natural ability to work with figures. Many years later he was earning a modest income as an accountant. The youngest brother, Sam, did well in his exam grades at school and college. He had no idea what work he wanted to do for a work career, but he had a strong work ethic and managed to earn an income as a went through life, but with several different career changes. The middle brother, Richard, didn't do particularly well in his school and college exams. Not that he wasn't intelligent. It was just that studying didn't interest him. What he did have was an inner vision that someday he would be a successful builder and property developer. With tunnel vision and determination to keep to his vision he did study for builders' qualifications. After working as an apprentice whilst he learnt his trade, he went on to establish his own building company. He kept the inner drive and determination to achieving his vision which was now to become successful with his building and property development company. He eventually became a wealthy man and his company employed a huge number of people as it acquired new housing and office development contracts. Richard was the most successful of his brothers simply because he kept to his tunnel vision end goal, knowing exactly what he wanted to achieve in life.

Our Angel Guides will help us to achieve our dreams, provided that they are realistic. Often, our inner visions are seeded in our Life Plan that was set before we were born. An important lesson is that Heaven will help us achieve our goals, our visions, provided that they are good and do not hurt others. We should keep to our visions with a determination to not be knocked off course because that mistakes it easier for Heaven to put things in place to help us along the way.

CHAPTER ELEVEN

Life Plan Readings

When I perform a Life Plan Reading I firstly sense that my Guardian Angel starts by brining messsages in the form of a clairvoyant reading, and to perform a psychic evaluation:

Has the client a history of any self-destructive behaviour patterns in life up to now? Such behaviour pattern can often be having relationships with someone who is controlling and self-centred. Will someone seeking a happier future life go against a possible happier future by committing to another relationship that will bring so much stress?

I have given Angel message readings for many people who have been in one or more relationships where they have been the victim of psychological abuse, and sometimes physical abuse.

A person might be attracted to another who seems to be self-confident and strong. Unfortunately, "Self-confident" is in reality "Self-centred" and a "Strong character" can turn out to be someone who is prone to a quick temper and anger. I usually find victims of such relationships coming to myself as a psychic for a look at their personal future with questions such as: "When will my future become better?; "Will I ever meet the right person?".

Our happier and more fulfilled future might be partly seen,

almost like it has been pre-planned. Such futures that are visions of a possible "Life Plan" can happen, but we need to make changes within ourselves from the past lessons. Otherwise our future will be a repeat of past.

Having been in a self-centred relationship and subject to bullying and control, we need to think closely about our feelings. Would we really trust that another overly self-confident person, who seems strong because he or she is prone to anger, will be totally caring and loving about ourselves?

Choosing a relationship with a totally different character, who is caring, might not fit our basic instincts, but could provide a happier, safer future.

The Angels know our pre-planned future, our predetermined Life Plan and work through our feelings. They communicate by giving us intuitive feelings and messages. Intuitive messages and visions about the future can be experienced by almost anyone.

The following true account is interesting in the way that a life can be dramatically changed by spiritually analysing a person's life in recent years to bring about a much brighter and positive future:

I was called to a home in Hull to give several readings, to a bunch of family and friends who had booked me. Halfway through the evening I was invited into a room to read for a lady in her late sixties. I had met these friends gathered in the lounge, and then one at a time walked through to the kitchen/diner to give each a private reading. The room this lady was sat in was in between the lounge and kitchen. It was reasonably big, decorated in the flowery wallpaper so popular in the 1970s. This was the year 2006. I noticed that there was no window in the room, but it was bright and clean. She looked happy, but as I started to give her a reading I felt very much that her life was on hold. I immediately saw a man with her in spirit who I knew was her husband. I told her this, she nodded to confirm, when I was then given a picture of a scene of a hospital bed. The same man was laid there with full life support systems attached. A doctor was in this scene looking past me at the lady I was with, asking her permission to switch off the life support. The doctor was telling her that there was nothing more the medical professionals could do. Her husband was technically brain dead, but his body was being kept alive by the machines. I gently told the lady what I was seeing. She remained calm and told me that her husband had died six years earlier. The doctor had indeed asked her permission to switch off the life support. She couldn't say yes, so went for a walk around the local streets. She had then walked back into the ward still unable to bring herself to give permission. Suddenly she just came out with the words necessary, giving permission for the life support to be switched off. The lady had remained calm whilst she told me all of this. She then became quite emotional, and said, "I murdered him. I murdered him. I have locked myself away in this room for the past six years. I haven't been out. I am looked after by my family, but I won't go out. I killed my husband." Her emotional outburst shocked me, but only momentarily. I was instantly taken back to the hospital ward. I had a bird's-eye view of her returning after her walk. I could see and hear her asking for the doctor, still undecided what to do, when suddenly her husband appeared, stood alongside her in spirit whispering in her ear "Switch off the life support. I am ok, I am free of my wrecked body, please tell him you give your permission, my love". The vision disappeared and I sat facing this emotionally distraught lady sat in front of me. I told her what I had just seen. I told her that her husband had not really been lying there in the hospital bed but was stood alongside her in spirit asking her to tell the doctor to switch off the life support.

The clairvoyant visions closed down as I sat opposite this lady. She slowly lifted her drooping head and stared at me eye to eye. Then a smile appeared. "You couldn't have known all of this. I now believe that my husband still exists. I did the right thing. I made the right decision."

I was then ushered out of her room to give another reading in the kitchen to a friend who had been waiting. At the end of the evening I walked into the lounge to say goodbye to everyone. The air of excitement was electrifying. A middle-aged lady who must have been the daughter said, "Mum has told us she is no longer grieving, she is no longer blaming herself for Dad's death. She wants to get her life going again. Her first request is that I take her out shopping tomorrow. Thank you for what you have done. You have no idea what a miracle it is to see Mum wanting to live her life again." I said goodnight, feeling very much that something much bigger than me was at work. I can't perform miracles but overwhelmingly felt humbled to be a part of something so life changing.

What we may become will be shaped by our future experience

LIFE GUIDE

Our Life Guide shows how we believe people should live their lives to gain a better place in Heaven.

Most ordinary people go to Heaven at the end of physical life. We can earn a "Better Place" in Heaven if we live our lives in a certain way.

When we say "Better Place", then for all of us "Heaven" is a beautiful place to be. However, we are still shown the mistakes we made, and in particular shown where we hurt others. Hurting others may have been either psychological hurt, or physical harm that we caused. Even the mostly good and caring people can accidentally or unintentionally hurt others at times, for such is the difficulty in living in our world. However, it seems to be that deliberate hurt is the most serious wrongdoing.

If we were guilty of deliberate hurt, pain and harm against others in our life then this may be presented before us by Wise Beings in Heaven, who want us to learn. They can, if they so decide, make us intensely aware of how the hurt we caused impacted on our victims.

In First Heaven we are also shown the good things that we did, the help and care we gave to our families, and others, and our care for animals and nature.

So, First Heaven is as beautiful and loving as you might expect, and a place for learning, and reflection on the life we just had.

My research shows absolutely that there is a God or "Source" of infinite intelligence, unconditional love, but you don't have to believe. You can live through a lifetime as a non-believer, and your place in the spiritual realm of Heaven is still waiting for you. You don't have to earn it, although you will be side-tracked if you are truly evil.

My research shows that the physical universe, and all of life and nature were deliberately created. Again, you do not have to believe this. It doesn't matter if you are a sceptic, or total non-believer.

My research shows that Evolution also took place. Similar forms of life in plants and animals did adapt through the laws of survival, changing to fit the climate, habitat and food sources of where they lived.

Evolution has also seen deliberate intervention at specific points in time by those that worked in the Creator's purpose to create new life and bring about totally new species.

Whatever we do in life, however we live our lives, the most important rule of living is to be caring and loving of others, of animals, of nature and of our planet.

Soulmates

The term "Soulmate" describes a spiritual connection between two people that precedes this life. We may meet our soulmates

in this life, and we may have more than one.
Often our friends and family may not be spiritual soulmates. When we do meet a soulmate there is an instant understanding between one another. There is a feeling of having a spiritual connection, and both of you feeling the same way, and being on the same level in a way that words cannot describe. This doesn't mean that such a person will be a partner to us in life, for often soulmates meet and then move on in separate directions.

The most intense soulmate relationship is where such a person is a partner or family member

Our Soulmates preceded our life, for we were with them in Heaven before we were born. Meeting a soulmate can be an important event in our Life-Plan. If it is, then our Guardian Angels will enable this, by putting a series of events in place in our lives to make our meeting with our soulmate just happen!

Angelic People

We should judge people by their actions, rather than what they say they might do.
Often, people may promise to help others, and promise to care, but their words never become actions.
There are some people who just "Get on" with helping others in spiritual love and care. They are so dedicated and caring towards others that they almost seem Angelic.
Our research has discovered that people who show spiritual love, and physically help and care for others often have an Angel working closely with them.
In everyday life our Guardian Angel stands back from us, and helps us when necessary, provided that we do not block our Angel through our self-centred Free Will.
When we are truly doing something that is spiritually loving and caring towards others then our Angel comes closer in order to help us and pass into us spiritual energies of the right kind.
If we are trying to help someone who is sick then our Guardian Angel will channel healing energies through us.
If our heart is pure, and we are dedicated in helping others, then sometimes our Angel will meld with us to become one with us. Such people may feel energised in body and in purpose. Others looking on may describe that person as "An Angel" because of their self-sacrifice and care for others.
It isn't just in helping people that our Angels work. They also work through people who actively help and care for animals, for nature, and for the environment of planet Earth.

HEAVEN

Guardian Angels do not abandon us when our life is at an end. They work hard to care and comfort us towards the end of life, and then reveal themselves to us when we leave our physical body. We pass into a most beautiful light, and then find ourselves moving through a portal towards the other side of life. We move towards a place that I call "First Heaven". This is a place where most ordinary, and basically good people pass across to at the end of life's days in the physical. Most people do not have to earn their place in the Spiritual Realm of Heaven. Our main Guardian Angel meets us at the gateway to Heaven, and guides us forward into the realms of Heaven.

There are other Heavens, but I feel it important to tell the world about First Heaven, because it is the place most ordinary people without strong religious beliefs go to after so called "death". If you have your own religious faith, then your religion will teach you about their Heaven.

First Heaven is surprisingly solid and much more real than the physical world around us. There are beautiful valleys, rivers, trees and flowers in radiant bloom of most vivid colours. We are free of pain, and emotional suffering. We may realise that First Heaven is a familiar place like going home. We were there before we were born. We may be given a beautiful garden to rest. We may be given a place similar to our home to rest and feel at ease whilst we adjust to our new spiritual state, now free of our physical body with all of its pain.

Loved ones who have passed before us may wait for us there, and we can find the joy of being re-united with them.

First Heaven is a "Gateway" to the further Heavens. For those with their own religious faiths then there are other "Gateways" that are described and taught by their faith.

People who were evil in life do not go to First Heaven but are side-tracked elsewhere.

In First Heaven
The Light above us is a "Sky" of gentle white light, yet whiter than any shade of white you can imagine. There is a "One"

whom people may call "God", "The Source", "The Creator".
The "Oneness" of the universe, of all spiritual beings, is felt very strongly in First Heaven, a place of unconditional love. We are loved for who we are, no matter what our faults. Love is the air we breathe.

In First Heaven we can appear as we did in life with our human body. Our true self is an orb of Light and Conscious Energy, so we can also appear as that.

Communication in First Heaven is by pure thought. We instantly know what is being communicated to us, and we can talk/communicate through our thoughts.

In First Heaven we can rest if our soul needs to build up energy again after a hard life. We can also be busy and continue learning.

We very much see, and are accompanied by the "Guardian Angels" who helped us through life, and other Higher Angelic Beings.

From First Heaven our Guardian Angels may help us look-on at those whom we love that are still in life. We can be seen by those with a gift of clairvoyance. We are not "Ghosts" when we are in First Heaven. Ghosts are something different.

LIFE REVIEW

We are given a "Life Review" in First Heaven. This is done in a loving way to see what we achieved, or to examine where we went wrong. Our lives are given to us for "Adventure", "Experience" and "Learning". The end goal is to hopefully become less self-centred, and more caring, loving and giving to others. This leads to spiritual growth.

We are shown in a loving way the mistakes and harm we may have caused to hurt others in life. We are also shown our achievements.

From this we can see that the most important lesson whilst still in life is to be loving and caring towards other people, and towards animals, nature, all of life, and the planet we live on.

Should we have done wrong it is a good idea to think about it now whilst in life, and to contemplate the errors we made. If we can try to make amends by becoming more loving and caring, this is much better than not bothering until we pass across to First Heaven.

Have you ever had a moment in your life where you could see your life clearly?
Have you ever thought: "What regrets will I carry at the end of my life? What will I wish I had done?"

A brief moment in time when we can stop in our busy lives and experience a moment of wonderful, intense clear thinking!

We may suddenly see one thing or several things that we should start to do. Things that will be positive experiences in our life that we never had time to do.
You see, in Heaven we are able to look back on our lives and review what we did. Heaven is a beautiful place, full of love. However, it is in this life where we can find adventure and raw experience. It is in this life that we can write a new page of our life diary each new day.

Our Guardian Angel may get through to us in moments of clear thinking, showing us things that we could be doing to maximise our life fulfilment. We should grasp these special moments with an intensity of purpose, and bring changes into our life as soon as possible!

LIFE PLAN ANALYSIS
further explained

Life Plan Analysis is a new way of seeing the future for individual people.

As a clairvoyant I find it easy to see some things in the future for a person that I am giving a reading. However, while these things I see are always good, positive things that a person would want, I realise that the same person might still be going through life difficulties, things going wrong in their life that seem terribly unfair.

When I see a person's future, images appear in my mind's eye. The mind's eye can also be called the "Third Eye". The images appear in a way that is familiar to all of us. For example, if I say "Visualise Big Ben in London", even though you might have never been there, you will have seen photos or video of Big Ben, and an image might appear in your mind.

As a clairvoyant I see images of the future of things that are not familiar to me, but absolutely relate to the person I am reading. It could be a new home, a new car, or an image of a person whom they are yet to meet in a new friendship. It could be a place they might travel, a new job, or success in sport, or artistic achievement.

The images come into my mind easily, but some fortune tellers might use visual aids such as cards, a crystal ball, or even reading tea leaves!

Life Plan Analysis give a much deeper reading
This is because much of our life up to now, and much of our future life is determined in the past.

Past Lives

As a human soul we were at some point in the distant past born out of the Spiritual Oneness of the Source of all Conscious Energy.

The Spiritual Dimension is a very real dimension. It is our true home. Our soul, the person whom we are, is made of conscious energy, and so the Spiritual Dimension of Heaven is our familiar home from where we came, and to where we return after each life.

I believe that soul energy has been around throughout infinity, and yet gives birth to new individual souls who are given many lives in the physical universe. For most of us the recurring lives are on Earth as human beings.

The reason for human beings having many lives seems to be complex, but driven by some very simple principles. These are:
To have adventure and experience.
To gain an identity. In Heaven we are an individual soul, living with other souls, and the air that we breathe is unconditional love. On Earth we are given a name, an identity, and we carve out our own path of success or failure.
It would seem that the most important reason for our life is to learn to love and care for others, and for animals and nature. This is the only way that we will spiritually grow. People who have no empathy, no consideration for others will not spiritually grow, and will stay at the same soul level, or even go back to an earlier level of soul development if they have been bad to others whilst in life.

We might have started our first life 100,000 years ago and lived through many lives. Once we are at a sufficient stage in our spiritual development we will reach a point where we don't have to go back into a life again. We will have other work to do in the Spiritual Realm.
Many of us will have started our life journey as recent as several hundred years ago. We will still have many future lives to come.
The time between lives can be several hundred years, or we can be reborn as frequent as twice per century. Many souls in Heaven have wanted to be back in life through the latter part of the 20th century, and early 21st century due to the different experience that science and technology has brought about. They all want the experience of travel by car and plane, computers, TV, mobile phones, and a less physical struggle compared with the primitive rural lives they might have had in the past. That is why there are over seven billion people alive today.

An interesting thing can be pointed out: Those who don't care about the planet and climate change don't realise that future generations will probably include a reincarnated life for them, so they will also suffer as reborn souls.

There are many true accounts of readings that I have given concerning how our past lives affect our present life.

Kelly (not her real name) came to me for a reading. Without her saying anything I immediately picked up that she had at least three long-term relationships that had ended badly. I also could see that she presently didn't have a close relationship.

Kelly immediately responded by saying "You are correct. Why does this always happen to me? Why can't I have a long-term, happy relationship?"

I added to my reading by seeing that her first relationship by marriage was very brutal. She had been subject to mental and physical abuse. She confirmed that, and almost broke down in tears.

I knew I had to get to the cause of these recurring relationship problems, so I clairvoyantly focussed on her immediate past life. I saw that she had been a woman (sometimes we have different genders in different lives), and that she had been married happily for over forty years. Her marriage in this past life was full of love, and she had been a mother to several children. I then saw a vision of her husband in this past life and compared it with the vision of her three failed relationships in this life. That's the answer! In this life she had instinctively been attracted to men with similar appearance, similar physical qualities to her husband in the past lives. This instinctive attraction had overridden the personality problems of her three failed relationships who had all treated her badly and each hurt her in their own way.

I told her the conclusions that this Life Plan Analysis reading had given. She sat there for a minute, saying nothing, and absorbing what I had said. "You are right," she said. "It all makes sense!"

I advised her to look at the personal, character qualities of any future partner. Some weeks later I saw her again. She is now in another relationship with a man she says has a pleasant character and is genuinely caring. She seems really happy.

Our Life Plan was determined in Heaven before we were born

We will emerge from a life on Earth back in our familiar home of Heaven having been shaped by our most recent life, and still carrying our experiences from previous lives.
We will have gained yet another identity, a new name, in our last life. We will need a period of adjustment, a period of orientation now we are back in the spiritual realm of Heaven.
Most souls go to a place that I name "First Heaven". I go into further detail of First Heaven elsewhere in this book, but it is best described as a place with similarities to Earth. There are beautiful flowers, trees, and all of nature resplendent in a landscape of valleys, vivid green grass, streams, and even houses. People may appear as they did in life, usually in middle age or younger. Our Guardian Angel accompanies us during this time, when we are also given a Life Review to see our life, almost like a video. During the Life Review will we see the good things that we did, our mistakes, and the hurt we may have caused others.
It also happens that in addition to adventure and experience during our physical life we are also measured on our ability to love and care for others, including all of life in animals and nature.
In First Heaven we can look-on at loved ones who are still alive in the physical. This is when people such as myself, a clairvoyant,

can make a connection and bring messages. Such connection is via Guardian Angels. The word Angel interprets as "Messenger". After a long period of time in First Heaven (although there is no such thing as time across there, only the moment of "Now"), we move on towards further learning and experience in other areas of Heaven. We will re-unite with our true soulmates who were born as a soul at the same time as ourselves. We may talk to each other to share our individual experiences in our lives on Earth. We may have met at least one of our soulmates in life, been a friend with one of them, or even shared a life as a partner or family member with a soulmate.

At some point we will be encouraged to move forward and agree to being born again into another life as a human being. This isn't forced on us, especially if our previous life was painful or traumatic. Our soul is given a chance to rest and rebuild our soul energy.

Before we go into a new life our Life Plan is drawn up by our Guardian Angel, together with other wise beings. These beings are like people, but spiritual beings who have lived through many lives and are now teachers.

Our Life Plan will address our character deficits from a perspective of developing our soul to be more loving and caring of others whilst in life. Our Life Plan can build-in the interests we may wish to develop, the work we might do, and the people we are destined to meet.

Life Plans will always include Life Challenges which are never easy but are not meant to cause personal suffering.

Free Will is destined to influence our day-to-day decisions, yet the major events and people we are destined to meet on our Life Plan will still happen, no matter what our free will decisions do to our lives.

Some souls volunteer for a life where they will have some physical disability, or a particularly tough life. This is because our souls learn more rapidly and spiritually develop to a higher level through hardship and struggle. If we are still able to be caring and loving towards others when our life is tough then we are truly spiritually bigger and stronger, and that's what Heaven seems to want of us.

LIFE PLAN READING

Whenever I give someone a Life Plan Reading it is usually to see what the future holds for them.
Much of our life up to now, our present, and our future, was planned-out in Heaven before we were born.
With the absolute help of my Angel Guide I clairvoyantly scan the past lives of a person, and then move on to scan the time in Heaven when their Life Plan for this life was being worked out and drawn up.
I'll give you a true example:
Richard came to me for a Life Plan reading. He had been through a divorce and was concerned for his children so shared custody with his ex-wife.
He was in some ways lonely, and needed to find a new friendship, a new partner, but his divorce had meant giving his home up to his ex-wife, and short of money for moving on, and no time for finding new friends.
I started by clairvoyantly scanning his past lives. When I clairvoyantly scan like this, I mainly pick up feelings of how a person was in past lives. I could see he had been quite selfish in his past lives and had only thought about his own needs. This had meant that others around him had been psychologically hurt by his lack of care.
Then came the Life Review whilst in Heaven before his present life. I could see that being selfish had held back his spiritual growth. He had agreed with the wise ones who put together his Life Plan that he would try to be more caring of others next time.
I then clairvoyantly scanned his life up to now. I could see that he had clashed with his ex-wife because she was and is very self-centred. He wanted to be there for his children in sharing

custody. He seemed determined to work hard at being genuinely caring, not putting himself first.

I explained my clairvoyant assessment to him, and he agreed with the findings.

I further explained that he was going through a period of his life when the interests of the children, and the needs of the children to still have a caring father, were more important than his own personal wishes, and he agreed.

Looking to the future for him I could see a vision of a future partner, an improved financial position and new home. The timeline of the vision coming to fruition was, however, several years hence. He said he was happy at that. He felt justified in his present lifestyle of some self-sacrifice for the benefit of his children and was so impressed at the accuracy of the reading that he felt he could now feel less anxious about his present life. I saw him several times, and each time he felt he was becoming spiritually calmer, stronger and wiser, and that he was less depressed and coping with everyday life much better.

What about things that happen to people to prevent life fulfilment?

Wars, accidents, pandemics, and other events that lead to human severe suffering are not usually on a person's Life Plan. Lives cut short by such tragedies see a soul return to Heaven earlier than planned.

The first process in Heaven is to give a soul rest, counselling, and a chance to rejuvenate their soul energies. A Life Plan can be picked up again, perhaps modified, and made ready for a new life once a person feels ready to enter another life.

Heaven is always viewed as a safe retreat for us, a familiar home where we truly belong. However, the lack of any memory of Heaven, combined with the cold, painful hardships of life leave us as human beings reluctant to accept that those in Heaven exist, let alone truly love us.

Also, many people have a terrific passion for life, and work hard towards achieving success in education, sport, music, art, and business. In addition, many people build up a family, and life seems at its most harsh when any tragedy strikes.

The Life Challenges that are set for us on our Life Plan are not life tragedies. Also, no matter whom we are as a soul our Life Plan may be severely restricted by others around. We may care for someone with a disability for many years and put our own dreams aside. This is where we surrender our free will to help others. This is of course spiritually positive and will help our continued soul development.

We may live in a society that restricts personal freedoms, or we might find ourselves poor in an affluent society where money rules. Both are examples of how our Life Plan might not attain fulfilment.

A Life Plan Reading can change our future towards a path of fulfilment.

As a clairvoyant my dealings with my clients is almost like no other. I have given over 6000 readings in the past fifteen years, and I cannot ask them questions. All that I do is an initial greeting, and yes, I do ask them their first name.

During the reading I simply ask the client if what I am telling them is correct. Very occasionally a client might say "No, that's not correct". I am always prepared to discontinue a reading at that point because I know I trust in what I am seeing clairvoyantly, but sometimes people don't want to hear the truth. However, through experience I can usually explain further what I am seeing, and that almost always helps the reading to be continued.

So, here is what might seem to be a problem. A person wants to see a better future, and yet here I am giving them a clairvoyant reading.

The clairvoyant reading helps me assess what is really going on in a person's life, and also helps them, as my client, to see and feel the miracle of clairvoyance. "There is no way that you could have known that!" is often said to me by the client.

The miracle of clairvoyance, and to me it is a miracle, will help me see anyone in spirit who wants to give a message, and it helps me see the current and past life situation of the client.

It is when I am giving the client details of their current and past life situation that I often find the client wanting to know more about what the future holds for them.

I can move the client into a Life Plan reading seamlessly, and very quickly look at their past lives clairvoyantly. I then ask my Angel Guide specific questions, in my mind thoughts, concerning the Life Plan of my client. My Angel Guide works with the Angels that accompany my client.

The questions I ask can typically include: Is the unfair and difficult time in my client's life now at an end? What better future can my client have? What are the hopes and dreams of my client, and will these be achieved in the future?

At this point on the reading assessment I can explain to the client all that I have been given in clairvoyant messages and visions. I then "Block" any unwanted things that could happen in my client's future should he or she simply carry on as they are with life. I then explain to the client the positive things that will come into their life, and as I explain the good things, such as a new friend, a new job or career, a new home, or perhaps fulfilment in sport, art, or music, I can see that a process is underway of actually changing their future Life Path for the better.

The following is a true case:

Linda came to see me. I could see her deceased mother in spirit. The love bond between them was strong and I brought through a lot of information from her deceased mother, including a message to not feel guilty for not being by her side when she unexpectedly passed. This message was received emotionally by Linda who was overjoyed to have re-united with her mother for those few minutes. I might have ended the reading there, but I was seeing visions of her life and that she wasn't completely happy. She was happily married with two children but couldn't understand why she felt deep-down unhappy.

I reviewed her past life where I picked-up that she had been a musician, playing the piano, and her best friend in her previous life, a female, had been one of her soulmates who was also a musician. I reviewed her life up to now, and she had money, a happy family, everything most people would want, but hadn't given herself any space for her own interests, the main one of which was music.

I then asked for visions of her Life Plan. I could see that if she took up music as a hobby, and took time to learn a musical instrument then she would find long-term fulfilment and she would also meet her sou-mate again, and a close friendship would happen.

Linda was amazed at the revelations from her Clairvoyant and Life Plan reading, and excited to be on a new path of life fulfilment, now very determined to allow herself time for her own passion in music.

CHAPTER TWELVE
Past Lives

When I am giving an Angel messages reading, I might be shown future positive events for someone. These are always impressive and such readings are meant to help people move forward with their lives in a positive way.

I always sense other underlying factors at play in a person's past, present, and future life. Finding out what these factors are can help give a much clearer view of our individual futures.

When giving someone a reading I often see that there could be a choice of futures. I needed to know what Angel guidance could be given someone to help them live a more positive, happier and fulfilling future.

I was a Christian until aged 55. I thought that my clairvoyant spiritual visions and messages from the Angels were religious experiences, even though many years of spiritual research were revealing a different picture to the teachings of my faith. Most Christian faiths disapprove of anyone having visions, and I eventually had to be sincere to myself in quietly stepping down from my Christian work which at that time was as a trainee Methodist preacher.

I now believe that we all have experienced many past lives. Christian beliefs are in our one life only, and to strive towards salvation through our beliefs, actions and deeds in this life.

Although I now know that we, as an eternal soul, have many lives, I am still passionate about living this life as if it were the only life that we have.

Past Lives can sometimes be identified through a personal hypnotherapy consultation.

Some clairvoyants, including myself, can pick up on a person's immediate past life, and even some previous past lives.

Our past lives have helped make us into the person we are in this life and continue to influence our present life in many ways.

Inner feelings that we can't explain could be caused by a previous past life.

The following is a true account, but with the person's name changed.

I gave Katie a reading. I had never met her before, and she appeared to be around the age of 60 years. I immediately felt the pain of a recently broken relationship, and she confirmed that as being correct.

I asked her to say nothing and told her that I could see that she has three adult children, and that the father was from an earlier relationship break-up.

I could also see a partner in spirit, with her, and he was very apologetic concerning his behaviour in the latter part of their relationship.

Katie confirmed that she had been through three marriages, and that all three husbands had turned to drinking excess alcohol, and became selfish, and aggressive. She had to pull away from each of the marriages.

"Why does this always happen to me!" came as an outburst from Katie.

The partner who had died was with her in spirit, and confirmed that he had been her second husband, and after 14 years of happy marriage had suffered a major personality change after becoming an alcoholic.

He was sorry for his selfish behaviour. I passed this message on to Katie, and she then told me that her marriage with him had been the "Best".

I couldn't explain "Why this is always happening to her" in an immediate clairvoyant assessment.

However, my Angel Guide, who helps me during clairvoyant readings, started to give me visions of Katie's past life. She had been happily married in her past life, and I began to see that in her present life she had been attracted to men with similar looks to her husband in her past life. She had just "Felt" that a prospective partner was right for her, based on his looks, not knowing why, and disregarding a future partner's character defects.

Being a different gender in a past life can be an explanation for our feelings in this life

The following is a true account, but with her name changed.

Linda, age mid-twenties, came to see me for a reading. She was, and is, openly a lesbian, and admitted that her true feelings had emerged after having some unpleasant relationships with men in her teenage years.

Linda had a massive anger problem and felt that she couldn't conform with school and education when younger and was now unemployed and unable to focus on a career.

She was looking for a loving relationship with another woman, but as yet was unable to find true happiness.

At first my clairvoyant assessment of her gave nothing much to say only that her grandfather came through in spirit to give some simple messages.

Suddenly, my Angel Guide gave me a vision of a young man, aged 19 years, in a battle. It was World War Two, and he was fighting alongside his comrades when they were hit by an artillery shell. The first experience he had was of his soul being thrown out of his body, and himself in spirit being pulled into the Light of Heaven.

We leave anger and stress behind before we reach Heaven. Even so, his regret at having his life cut short, of not experiencing a long and loving relationship with a girlfriend carried in his memory.

Once reborn into a new life in the 1990s, as a female, named Linda, he had lost his memory of his immediate past life. However, the anger re-emerged, and his search for a loving female relationship eventually started to dominate him, now as Linda.
Upon communicating this vision to Linda, she immediately felt that at last there was an explanation for her anger, and for not being interested in a career. She felt that she had at last realised who she was, and is. She will continue looking for a happy, loving, lesbian relationship, and hopefully find some employment career, now knowing how her past life has affected her present life in such a big way.

As we progress through many lives we naturally want to ask: "Why do we have lots of lives?"
Living lives for the adventure and experience are certainly some of the main reasons.

Those in Heaven see the Grand Purpose of our lives as becoming more caring and loving towards others, animals, nature, and our beautiful planet, and being less self-centred.

It would seem as though younger souls are naturally more self-centred, and more mature souls become more loving and caring to others.
I have considered this carefully in my research over many years and come to the conclusion that for Heaven to survive, those souls dwelling there must be loving and caring to each other. It's a feeling of Oneness.
This feeling of Oneness is so strong in Heaven that as we become aware of how we hurt others, and hurt nature, then we start to realise that we are equally hurting ourselves.

Planet Earth has a large number of younger souls. This is self-evident in self-centred behaviour, and lack of empathy towards others, that is widespread.

Mature souls are more loving and caring. They may sacrifice many of their own worldly pleasures to help others, and nature. So, our present and future life is being determined by our spiritual progress. This can be identified clairvoyantly.

Between Lives – Life Review and next life planning

At the end of each life our soul, the person that we may call "I" or "Me", leaves our physical body, and returns home to Heaven.

After many years of giving Angel messages readings, I realise that we carry across there not only our character, but also our memories.

When reading to connect with someone who suffered from dementia, I find that spiritually retained memories only go as recent as immediately prior to the onset of their dementia.

We do not carry serious emotions, stress, anger, worry, or sorrow across with us. We leave these behind as we find ourselves entering the spiritual realm of pure, unconditional love.

When we leave our physical body we will find ourselves seeing our Guardian Angel, probably for the first time. Our Guardian Angel will appear as a person, but radiant with soul energy. We will not feel afraid, but instinctively know that this is a Being of love.

Most people, most souls, pass across to Heaven after their physical life is at an end.

I call this place "First Heaven" because it is the first place we travel to.

First Heaven is very real and solid. The immense beauty and vivid colours are beyond description.

There are fields, trees, flowers, rivers and lakes. There may also be homes, similar to a home where a soul may have lived on Earth.

I describe First Heaven in more detail elsewhere in this book. However, we will have many things to do. These include re-uniting with our soulmates, a Life Review, looking at our Life Lessons and spending time with Wise Beings in the Afterlife who will assess our spiritual progress.

Planning our next life

Our next life is planned in Heaven before we are reborn. We will be aware of our future Life Plan and know the reasons why our future life will hold Life Lessons.
When we are reborn, the conscious memory of our time in Heaven is deliberately erased. However, our Guardian Angels know our Life Plan, and by becoming more aware of our Guardian Angels, and how they communicate through our feelings, we can be more in touch with understanding the reasons for our life experience in the past and present, and obtain a glimpse of our future Life Plan events yet to happen.
As a clairvoyant, I can pick up messages and visions of our future Life Plan events clairvoyantly with the help of our Guardian Angels.

Past Life behaviour will determine some of our present life experiences

Whilst in Heaven we will at some point experience a Life Review. This usually happens soon after our passing.
Our Life Review is in the presence of our Guardian Angel, and Higher Spiritual Beings, often appearing in human form.

A lot of emphasis is given on how much we helped others in our lives. This is classed as good and positive.

In situations where we were totally self-centred in our behaviour towards others, these situations will be brought to our attention. If we were lacking in empathy, and in situations where we deliberately hurt others emotionally or physically, then this is looked on as bad behaviour. We can be shown life situations in our life that has passed as if reliving them in real time, but this time feeling the hurt we may have caused.

How are we punished for bad behaviour?

Punishment isn't the correct way of describing the outcome of our bad behaviour. Heaven is a place of unconditional love and safety for all who make it there, and most souls do reach Heaven successfully.

After our Life Review, there is a realisation at a spiritual level of shared responsibility for each other. A feeling of "Oneness" of all souls, and that if we hurt another soul we are also hurting ourselves.

We eventually will volunteer for another life where we might agree to be a victim of someone who treats us badly, just as we hurt others in the past. This would be to give us an experience where we can learn. Our souls often grow more quickly in positive ways during hard times in life.

If we can endure our own difficult life, and yet still be caring towards others, then we are truly growing spiritually.

So, it can be seen that our past lives, followed by our Life Plan mapped out in Heaven, would have had a significant role to play in our current life. This often explains why some people's lives seem to have been harder than others.

The good news is that clairvoyantly we can identify these "Life challenges" set before we were born.

For all of us, learning to be closer to our Guardian Angels can help us "Feel" that we know our Life challenges.

In this book we are talking about seeing the future. As a clairvoyant I can see some of the positive future events for someone. I can also identify their life challenges which may continue to underly future happenings.

Life challenges can be analysed: Are these Life Lessons that are difficult to endure now at an end?

Can the Life challenges be avoided in the future and a person's life changed for the better? ***Absolutely, yes!***

Our future after this life – will be affected by our behaviour in this life

CHAPTER THIRTEEN

THE CLAIRVOYANT

This chapter is written to explain further what I see and experience as a clairvoyant who works with the Angels.
There is no scientific evidence of the eternal spiritual soul that we all are and have. It is the person inside whom we call "I" or "Me". That person inside has an eternal existence beyond our physical life.
Everything spiritual, including our soul, is of another dimension. That is why physical science cannot detect our soul and cannot detect Heaven.
Within ourselves, we are a soul of conscious, intelligent energy made of the same stuff as the energies of Heaven. Heaven is our true familiar home where we came from, and to where we return.
The human brain is most amazing. The brain has within the ability to link and meld with our soul energy. The neurons firing within the brain create energies that communicate with our soul energy so perfectly that we feel as one with our human body born into the physical world of Earth. The brain is a link with both the dimension of Heaven and Earth. Perhaps future discoveries of how this link works might provide some scientific evidence of the spiritual dimension.

What do I experience as a clairvoyant?
Well, firstly I try to ground myself in everyday life. I am a qualified accountant and have always worked hard in my career. I have hobbies and interests, and a passion for my main interest –

music.

Clairvoyance is something that I can switch-on when my mind turns to it.

When I am giving someone an Angel messages reading I sense their Guardian Angel communicating with my Guardian Angel. It is they who enable the readings to happen. I am given visions as images of people who have passed, of scenes in someone's life, of landscapes, homes, cars, and almost anything. The visions are always of relevance to the person I am helping through the reading. I also receive information, either as a sudden voice when I am given a name, or a sudden "knowingness".

What I do find consistently is that the readings only occur where there is a bond of love, family, or friendship, between the person in front of me and the person in spirit.

Throughout my life I have also been given visions of other things:

I can see across to Heaven.
The place I see is a place I call "First Heaven". This follows from my vision from the Archangel and is because this is the first place we go to after we pass across from our physical life.

I can see people who are in spirit where there is a love or friendship connection.

I can channel messages from their Angel Guide via my Angel Guide in the form of Visions, and messages as a voice or "Sudden knowingness".

I can see the Guardian Angels of people. I can communicate with Guardian Angels – I call them "Angel Guides".

I can see that Angels respond to our prayers to God. The Angels work on the instructions and in the purpose of God.

I can see Angels bringing healing to people. I can see the different colours of the energies Angels channel when bringing healing. I can help people myself with Angel Light Therapy.

I can see Life Plans, and some of a person's future. The future is also determined by our free will.

I can see Angels working in nature.

I can see, feel, and know the meaning of life.

ANGELS

As a clairvoyant I can see our Guardian Angels.
Millions of people believe in Angels. People across differing faiths, and those with no religious beliefs share a common belief in Angels.
Very few people have actually seen an Angel. Very few people claim to have received a message from an Angel. So what is the truth? Well, I hope in this book you may discover that each and every one of us has a Guardian Angel, and that Angels are constantly at work helping us through life.

Is it true that Angels help people all of the time? I can at times see through to the reality of Heaven, and I observe the Angels at work trying to help us. They are most definitely trying to help people all of the time throughout life.

In my work career I am a matter-of-fact accountant, and I had always sought to find the meaning of life, as many people do. In particular I wanted to make sense of what I was seeing and feeling with my clairvoyant gift. In my quest for knowledge I made an amateur study of quantum physics, astronomy, religions, philosophy, and in talking to people about their beliefs. I would be fascinated by ghost stories and would often talk to people who had suffered bereavement. Some people, especially where a couple had been happily married for many years and one spouse had died, would describe times when they could sense the deceased person with them.

How can we believe in God, Angels or anything spiritual?

Before we are born we are in Heaven, and when we die we go back to Heaven. So, heaven is a familiar place in our deep, innermost memories. When we eventually return there after our life on earth is over, it is just like going home.

However, and it is a big "However", our memories of heaven are deliberately erased when we are born. This might seem cruel, hard, and leave us wondering why.

If we could all remember heaven would people be more loving and caring of each other because they would know that they should not be hurting others.

If we could all remember Heaven then would we not simply end our own life when the going gets tough?

Well, the answer to this biggest question of all is to be found in the very reason we are given a life on earth as a human being in the first place. We are given life to EXPERIENCE, to LEARN, and to hopefully GROW. To "Grow" means to become less self-centred, and more loving and caring of others, of nature, and of the earth we live on.

LIFE PLAN. As described previously, before we are born we are given a "Life Plan". This includes things we will do, people we will meet. We have "Soul Mates" and we will certainly meet one or more of those on our "Life Plan". The joy of meeting a Soul Mate is something which we all deserve to experience. You may find so much in common with this other person, and you may get along so well that you may feel you have known that person all of your life. The truth is that you will have known them before this life, and that you were meant to meet and find each other again. We also have "Free Will" to live our lives as we feel we ought to, and do what we must do. Our Free Will often takes us away from the Path Of Life – our Life Plan. This is when life can become even more difficult.

Life is hard, so how can we believe that Angels exist to help us?

What about children who are suffering famine, and may die in childhood? What about people living in war zones or oppressive societies? What about children brought up in an oppressive family environment? What about those born with disabilities? Why, if there is a God does He or She allow so many people to have such difficult or tragic lives? Is it no wonder that so many people don't even have some religious beliefs?
Life on planet Earth can be beautiful, happy, full of love, or painful in extremes of emotional and physical suffering, human cruelty, and lacking in love.
Again, the answer is because the gift of life is meant to be an opportunity for all of us to experience pain and pleasure, experience relationships, love, hate, friendship, loneliness. We may all experience emotional pain and grief, and also happiness. We may experience adventure, we may all learn, explore. The Head of the Oneness, the Source that religions may call God, is a God of unconditional love, yet that love is indeed "Tough love" because we only GROW when the going gets tough. We only GROW through adventure, through experience, through learning. Certainly, we may take four steps forward and three steps back, yet all of our experiences in life are recorded in our spiritual memory and can be re-visited when our lives are at an end and we return to heaven.

HOW THE ANGELS HELP PEOPLE

I want to show you how the Angels try to speak to us through our intuition, which is the starting point of how they communicate. In the most extreme form, intuition becomes Clairvoyance, but very few people are clairvoyant. Most people know what I mean when I talk about intuition, and many are capable of acquiring some clairvoyant ability. Clairvoyance is actually *a series* of spiritual GIFTS, given to us as we develop spiritually in a positive way. I hope I can show you an insight into a whole new reality that will open up your spiritual development progressively. We all have different spiritual gifts, and I hope that many of you will learn how Angels communicate with us.

People in my audience often comment that they sense a calm, healing atmosphere. My Angel Guide shows me a vision of those who are spiritually very much alive in Heaven and will pass on messages to loved ones. I also am shown images of places and objects that may mean something to the person I am reading. I may also see what has happened, and what is happening in the lives of those whom I read, and ask my Angel to show me the Life Path for that individual, to help them back on the correct path to fulfilment and happiness.

Angels help in the following ways: As previously explained, Angels speak to us through our intuition. Have you ever struggled with a problem, unable to find an answer, then suddenly the answer is there? Have you ever been overwhelmed by stress and worry, and then somehow you work through the situation? Have you ever had a gut feeling that you shouldn't go somewhere, and later discover that you are glad you listened to your intuition? Maybe you didn't listen to your intuition and regretted doing something? Your Guardian Angel helps you through your intuition. There is no language, just an instant awareness of what we should or shouldn't do by a form of telepathy which we don't acknowledge because we don't realise that we are being helped. In some people the fine tuning of their intuition can lead to an individual becoming in some ways clairvoyant. If we pray to God for healing, then a Healing Angel will help bring healing directly to the person suffering, both spiritually, and through those working to help medically.

Angels can be with us to give us STRENGTH. Both physical, and emotional strength.

A Prayer to God is essential. Angels can be with us to guide us through life's problems and difficulties.

Angels helping us in our daily lives can only be appreciated if we believe in God and the Angels.

A word of caution: Angels rarely communicate as a voice in your head unless to give a sudden warning of imminent danger. A voice in your head is not allowed because a voice telling us what to do would go against our "Free Will" to live our lives as we choose. Also, an Angel of God would never be a nuisance by bothering you in ways you don't want. Angels of God certainly never guide us with bad thoughts.

Angels help all of us as we near the end of life, and when we pass across to Heaven.

I have had an account from a nurse who has worked in the resuscitation ward of hospital. She informed me that whenever she saw an Angel at the bed head of a patient she knew the patient was more likely to die. The doctors and her would inevitably have a more difficult time, but often still saved the life of such patients.

Angels who bring healing. A prayer to God can bring direct healing help through the Angels and help by bringing professional medical attention.

Angels to provide our basic needs of food, clothing, a friend to talk to.

What do you really want out of life? What do you need most to achieve fulfilment? Well. The Angels won't help you win the lottery, but they can offer a tremendous amount of help in achieving our goals, and fulfilment in life. What do we need to do? Well, the starting point is simply to be open-minded to a belief in

Angels!

How can a belief in Angels and Clairvoyance help you?

If you can find somewhere quiet where you can spend a few minutes on your own. It could be just another room in your home. Sit quietly, relax, and try, just try to blank your mind and think of nothing for just one minute. What can you achieve by worrying about the past or future? So, sit quietly and try to appreciate the intensity of the moment of "Now". Listen to any background sounds even in the quietness. Did you succeed? Remember, just no thoughts for one minute. In Heaven, time does not exist. There is only the "Now". Time is purely a physical thing….the revolution of the Earth, the hours in the day, the days in a year. We should learn to live more in the moment of the "Now", and appreciate every moment of our life as a gift from God even in the hardest of times.

Right, now as you sit quietly think about your most pressing problem at the moment. Quietly say a prayer to God, or think a prayer in your mind, and ask for help. Then, leave it at that. You have passed your problem up to God. Within minutes, hours, or a day or so you may be surprised how suddenly you become aware of an answer to your problem. Alternatively, you may just feel better about yourself, and the problem will be something that you find the strength and wisdom to handle.

This "Sudden answer" is real help from your Guardian Angel. So how has the Angel communicated? Well, by helping you, the feeling of being helped, the intuition that you receive. Clairvoyance gives you greater certainty that there is life after death. This helps you personally handle grief from bereavement better. You can never get over bereavement, yet you can get through it. It helps you see that your own life is just part of an eternal process of the life of your soul. Your soul is the bit inside of you that you know as "I" "Me". Clairvoyance can help people with problems in their lives. A psychic reading can help people with problems of finances, relationships, stress, ill health, worry, insecurity, lacking in fulfilment. Clairvoyance is useful in seeing situations surrounding people.

Telling them what you see as a clairvoyant often astonishes them and helps them believe. This opens their minds to showing them that they can receive spiritual love, strength, wisdom and support. It is even possible to look at their future life-plan to get them back on course.

Clairvoyance is mainly used to communicate with those who have passed across to "The other side of life". It is a way of helping people suffering bereavement through their personal loss and grief. In such times people are suddenly hit by the harsh reality of our human mortality. People often never think of anything more than just their personal everyday lives.

Clairvoyance provides evidence that there is a God, or if you prefer a different term, a "Divine Energy", and that we are indeed spiritual. This may help people start to change the way we live. If we try to live in accordance with spiritual laws that help us spiritually grow in this life, then we have a more positive experience when we pass into the afterlife. Clairvoyance allows us to see a vivid picture of First Heaven.

When I do an Angel Messages reading I see images, sometimes like still photos, and sometimes like a video. The images are of those who have passed, stood close to the person I am reading. This is often where there is a bond of love or friendship. I always put a block on seeing images of anyone who wasn't a friend or loved one. I seem to know what they are saying by some kind of transfer of thoughts. I don't hear voices or speak to the dead. I regard all those who make it safely across to this place which I will call "Heaven" as not being dead, but very much alive.

When trying to explain this I use the visual image of a car. When we see a car, then we may not see the driver inside. The windscreen can be reflective, leaving a view of the driver dark and unclear.

At the point of death of our physical body, to the real person inside it is just like getting out of a car. We stand outside of the car, and likewise stand outside of our physical body, look back and think "Was that me?" "I am still the same person".

LIFE CHANGING EXPERIENCES

Most life-changing experiences are quiet, personal ones. Earlier in the book I described how I felt a Guardian Angel with me when I was near death in hospital with asthma. However, as I grew older, into my teens, as with any normal teenager my mind forgot about spiritual experiences from my infancy. My subsequent life-changing experiences were quiet, personal ones. I wasn't suddenly going to change the world overnight by bringing to the world my vision, and a new way of life. No, the world doesn't change. Life hopefully continues. We should count each day as a blessing. We should think of the things we have in this life and be thankful. We should try not to become too depressed or consume ourselves with jealousy because of things we don't have. Earlier in the book I described a very real experience of a vision and a spiritual journey given to me by an Archangel on

1stMay, 1999. Over the weeks and months following my journey into Heaven I experienced visions of Light many times. I still do to this day. When the moments are more intense, I see the face of the Heavenly Being. His eyes always draw my attention. They have depths of infinite wisdom, understanding and unconditional love. Immediately after my journey to Heaven I knew I was being prepared to do some kind of spiritual work to help others. I could ask in my thoughts almost any question about the meaning of life, and the answer would be given to me. I was on a rapid learning curve. I learnt the power of prayer, and that non selfish prayers to God are listened to and answered, but not always with the answer we want!

The big negative is that life-changing experiences don't change the world around you. I still had to work for a living. I had family to keep, a mortgage to pay, and couldn't just drop everything for some spiritual adventure. I still struggled with all the pain and difficulties of normal life.

I broached the subject of spiritual experiences with friends. The boredom factor quickly set in whenever I tried to discuss my experience with my good friends who were normal mates. We enjoyed a good laugh and sharing each other's problems. If I began to talk about what had happened it just seemed weird to them.

I then had this idea that surely some people who went to Church must be drawn to religion because they had similar spiritual experiences. I started attending a fundamentalist Christian Church, but after several months realised I couldn't have been more wrong. I found out that the Holy Scripture says that the devil appears as an angel of light. Anyone who spoke of seeing angels was condemned for seeing the devil. It seems that religious miracles are with some faiths confined to 2000 years ago, and not permitted since. What about my spiritual gift of discernment between good and evil? In my visions I can discern between visions from Heaven, and the evil antics of demons, and negative energies. Holy Scripture teaches us about spiritual gifts as being "Fruits of the spirit". Every one of us has a gift, a talent, and discernment is a gift I have been granted. Why would I be criticised for simply being honest and truthful? We are all different. We should make the most of the talents and abilities. Also, we should not dwell on the gifts that we don't have but others do.

However, I didn't want condemnation by religious fundamentalists, so I told myself I wasn't going to allow myself to see ghosts. I wanted to try to use my spiritual gifts through normal channels, restricting myself in what I said and did, and conforming to Christian teachings. I moved to join another less fundamental Church and spent four years training to be a Christian preacher.

During those four years I was judged as a good preacher. I kept strictly to the Church doctrine and had a ready gift when it came to what is called "Exegesis". This is where we read a passage from Scripture and interpret the relevance in today's modern world. I wrote spiritual poetry, always including one of my poems in a service. During my four years preaching I led over 100 services. These were often commented on as being services with an atmosphere of healing. I would even get letters from members of the congregation commenting on how my service had given them a sensation of healing, even though I deliberately kept the services formal. The services were sometimes recorded and made available at the local hospital for patients to hear. My spiritual poetry received local acclaim, and I gave poetry readings on local radio, and was privileged to read my poems at events within the region.

The visions, however, kept appearing. I remember trying to console a bereaved widow in a Christian way, seeing clearly her husband stood with her, yet unable to comment or give her a message. Christian teachings in my Church were that the only people who went to Heaven were those who had been Baptised, accepted Jesus Christ as their Lord and Saviour, and led an active Christian Life within the Church, living a life of repentance and worship.

Conversations with Church Ministers, Vicars, Priests, and Pastors seemed to give no indication that they could see the things I was seeing. I felt sad at Vicars leading funerals for non-Christians with words indicating that the deceased would be in Heaven. Yet I knew the teachings of their faith meant they couldn't truly believe that the deceased had passed across to everlasting life in Heaven. After four years I quietly stood down from preaching. I believed in the work I had been doing as a preacher. Churches do teach people there is a God, and how we should live good lives. Churches also teach us to respect God, to repent for our mistakes, and live this life as if it were our only chance to get to Heaven. I have since learnt we have many lives, but that doesn't mean that this very life we are in now shouldn't be lived to the utmost in our caring for others, for nature, and the planet so that we may spiritually grow.

I was a Christian by religion, but I could no longer hold back the bigger picture and the work I had to do, however controversial. My true clairvoyant work was about to begin.............

Spiritual Understanding

We cannot gain Spiritual Understanding immediately. It can take a lifetime. A door to spiritual awareness is within each one of us. In many it remains closed throughout life. For some, as with myself, the door can be gradually opened.

It was the year 1966. I was age sixteen and a screeching of tyres, together with the roaring sound of an engine at maximum revs filled my ears. I was sat passenger in my mate's Mini 850cc as he drove it as if he were driving a rally car around the bends of the country roads surrounding our home village of Silsden in the Yorkshire Dales. He was seventeen and had just passed his driving test. The car had been acquired by my mate for next to nothing. I didn't ask if it was taxed, insured and properly serviced. After half an hour of clinging onto the seat just wishing I was driving and wishing I could drive like him we stopped outside of his house. The car looked worse for wear with shabby paint work, but in typical teenage banter I said, "Well it sure goes fast". We both stood admiring his pride and joy as he held a smile of satisfaction on his face. Suddenly there was a loud crack and a crash. The front wheel of the parked car just literally fell off and the front end crashed to the ground. "Oh! my! we've just been doing eighty miles per hour in that thing. We could have been killed," said I. He ran round to the front of the car, not really knowing much about cars. Not much knowledge about cars was needed as he pointed his hand at the front suspension and some rusted metal that had snapped. The car was on the scrap heap next day with my mate vowing to get revenge on the man who had sold him the car.

That very next day I was back at work at the office. I was a trainee accountant working for a prestigious firm of chartered accountants. Two of the bosses, known as "Partners", and both in late middle age, drove very nice cars indeed. One was an "E-Type"

Jaguar. The other had a new top of the range Rover.

I realised all of a sudden that when we look at a car we don't always see the person inside. A fast, new expensive car can be driven by a tired old man. An old, shabby small car can be driven by a younger man or woman at the height of their youthful looks and in their physical prime.

THE DOOR TO SPIRITUAL AWARENESS OPENED SLIGHLTLY. A realisation came over me that the real person inside each one of us is like the driver of a car. The thoughts came flooding in: A handsome or beautiful looking person might be uncaring, bad tempered, and self-centred. Another ordinary looking person could be totally caring and giving. When we die is it just as if we are a driver stepping out of our car? All the world ever saw was our physical body. The real "I" or "Me" inside is separate to our physical brain. Do we step out of ourselves at the end of physical life, look back and say: "Was that me?".

As these thoughts crossed my mind I sensed something bigger at work. A spiritual "Someone" was helping me open the door to spiritual awareness.

The very first lesson in the road to being clairvoyant is to actually accept that we are spiritual, and that another spiritual dimension or "Heaven" must exist. Opening this door to our beliefs is perhaps the most difficult because science tells us that we must find proof before we can accept anything as being real. How can we prove that we are of spirit? How can we convince our logical minds? After a lifetime of trying to find proof I realise that the spiritual world is another dimension. Scientific instruments are designed to take measurements in the physical dimension. It might be impossible for scientific instruments to measure the energies of another dimension.

So how can we ever prove anything spiritual? This can only be done by reaching logical conclusions from evidence that is totally convincing and withstands thorough investigation. The most convincing evidence is of course if we experience something supernatural ourselves.

CHAPTER FOURTEEN
Hauntings

Being "In Tune" with Heaven and able to sense our Guardian Angel gives ourselves access to the most powerful force in the universes of both the Spiritual Realm and the physical universe of our planet Earth. Negative energies that often cause hauntings exist in small pockets. The ability to be "In Tune" with Heaven protects us from fear and harm that evil can cause. When I attend a haunted building I can command the ghosts or whatever is there to "Be gone". For the strongest evil hauntings a Christian prayer is what is needed to get rid of the evil entities. Sometimes a ghost is just a traumatised soul that has stayed Earthbound. I can speak to them and I try to help them move on to Heaven.
I give true examples of the different types of hauntings in the following narrative.

A modern day haunting

I awoke to the sound of my alarm ringing out loud. It was pitch black. The alarm was an old clockwork wind-up type with no LED, so I struggled for the bedside lamp switch wondering what was going on. With a reassuring click I had light, and tried to focus my sleepy eyes, and then stared in bewilderment at the time – 3am. I had set the alarm for 7am, ready to get up for work, and the alarm dial still clearly pointed to 7am. My bedroom door was open, and I remember having closed it until the latch clicked as I always do. I mentally shrugged the incident off and soon fell asleep again.

The next evening just before 7 o'clock I closely examined this rogue alarm clock. I firstly experimented by setting the time to just before 3 o'clock, and kept the alarm pointer at 7 o'clock. These old wind-up alarms have just a 12 hour cycle. It worked as it should, with nothing happening at 3 o'clock, but then I reset to the correct time, and at 7 o'clock it rang. "Good!" I said to myself, quite confident that it wouldn't wake me up again at 3am.

I fell asleep as normal that evening. The bedroom was always very dark with no street lamps to give a hint of light. I awoke in pitch black again, this time to hear the sound of my bedroom door handle turning. No sooner had I awoke than the alarm rang out. I again fumbled for the switch of my bedside lamp. It was 3am and the bedroom door that I had so carefully closed was wide open with no-one around.

There was only one other person in the house. It was an elderly lady and I had just moved in as her lodger. I was age 20 years and had recently moved away from home. I mentioned the strange events to her over breakfast next morning. She immediately knew the answer: "Oh! that will be my previous lodger who died recently. He was disabled and lived with me for 10 years. He won't be very pleased that someone else is sleeping in his bed and has taken his place." I sat at the breakfast table in her kitchen in a moderate state of shock. The lady was entirely believable. I had moved in following her advert in a local newspaper for a lodger. Her home cooking was superb, and her motherly attitude was much appreciated by me as a young man away from home.

This was one of my first experiences of the supernatural. The alarm continued to ring on occasion at 3am, but not every night. I knew that the ghost of the lodger didn't mean any real harm, but to me was just annoying. This is a personal experience which defies rational explanation, and the comments from my landlady made perfect sense.

My friend at work was a very down to earth man, aged in his early forties. I could tell him anything and told him the story of my experience in my lodgings. He didn't believe in the supernatural, and just laughed at my story as most people would. However, he then quietly told me of his own strange experience when he had been on a stay in London. He had walked down a side street one evening, looking at some smaller shops, when he noticed a crowd stood around one particular shop window. It was a shoe shop, and the shoes were literally flying around all over the place behind the glass of the shop front. He describes the scene as if some invisible hand was picking them up and throwing them all over inside the shop front. It was early evening time and the shop was closed, and the display window brightly illuminated. No-one was reacting to this strange sight beyond comments such as "Just look at this". People stood staring for a while and just walked away. Perhaps they, just like my friend, didn't try to make sense of what they saw, which is how many of us react in such circumstances. The phenomena of an invisible "Something" throwing the shoes around seemed to fit a description of poltergeist activity.

Have you ever had an experience that could be described as paranormal?

Has a friend, or someone you know ever described a paranormal experience? Did you just dismiss it in the back of your mind with quiet thoughts of disbelief? Often we just assume that our friend who is totally reliable was just imagining their experience. Maybe there was a rational explanation that you would have picked up on if you had been there?

That is how we handle such information in our thoughts. It is normal to dismiss paranormal experiences because we are deliberately programmed at birth to not remember our spiritual past existence. How about realising this and making a decision to have a more open mind? You will be surprised at how this makes a further change in your life. You will have taken another step on your path of spiritual development.

THE BOOK OF LIFE

In our daily lives in the physical we are each day going through many experiences. Many of life's experiences are mundane, some are unpleasant, some are painful, hurtful, or experiences of fighting and hate. In contrast some experiences are happy, fun, or an experience that is an adventure. The most profoundly positive experience is that of love.

Each day we create a new page of the book of our life.

At some point in the future, when we have passed across to heaven, we can revisit those parts of our life we need to or want to. It is like turning to a certain page in a book. This is a book that we wrote, page by page, each day of our lives. We can jump into a video replay of that day that is so real that it is real to us. The days we choose to visit are those in which there were intense emotional experiences: either of happiness or sorrow, adventure and discovery or depression and despair; achievement, or loss.

When we go to a haunted house, often the haunting is the spirits of those who have lived in that house before. They are revisiting the place they want to visit, usually for some emotional reason. They are re-living different time periods and sometimes don't even notice you there in the present of today.

HAUNTINGS IN OLD BUILDINGS

There are several types of haunting and not all are the same. In February 2013, I visited one of the most haunted houses in York, on Stonegate, a well-known street in the main tourist shopping area. I was just a paying participant of an overnight vigil organised by one of the well-known companies who organise ghost hunting events. I arrived at 8pm for a 9pm start and was told to wait outside. Later, as the time approached 9pm I was surprised at how many people had booked to attend this evening. Entering this house with small rooms was a party in excess of 30 people, each paying over £50, so my first impression was of commercial greed compromising the ideal situation of a smaller number of participants in a ghost hunting vigil. However, the residual and active spiritual energies in this house proved fascinating. The first discovery I made was that several of the different types of haunting were very strongly manifest and provide excellent examples.

I kept quiet for an hour or so that I am clairvoyant... although it did come out before the night was over in quite a dramatic way. The guest clairvoyant was speaking about a monk, who haunted the house, because the site had once been a monastery. I could clairvoyantly see the monk who seemed quite harmless, stood in a corner. He remained harmless through the evening. However, as we were grouping together on the first floor, I clairvoyantly saw a wild-eyed man with unkempt black hair come charging through the door. He looked crazed. I asked my angel guide who he was. I was told that he had spent several years fighting overseas, around the late 18th century, and had returned home completely mad and quite violent. Back to the real world, and the ghost hunt leader was explaining that in this room objects were often thrown around. I knew who was throwing them but I said nothing.

So this is an example of a grounded spirit, still earthbound because the circumstances of his life had turned him into a madman. Why don't the angels rescue such souls? I don't have all the answers.

The group were next led downstairs into the cellar/ basement. As a group of around 30 people, we were all forced into a very tiny room area. I got myself positioned into a corner of the room. "This is at the level of the street in Roman times and is where Roman Legion soldiers in ghostly form have been seen marching." I clairvoyantly looked around for Roman soldiers, but there were none. Such apparitions usually concur with a date or a time of year when some emotionally charged event happened, in this case way back 2000 years ago. However, I did hear a voice whispering to me in some old language. It was a male voice, repeating the same words over and over again. Was it Nordic? ... the Vikings had captured and ruled over York. Was the language Roman, or even old English? I said to my angel guide in my thoughts "Please translate". The voice immediately became clear with the words "Help me", Help me", repeated over and over again. Was this some poor soul grounded for more than 1000 years? I didn't get chance to find out as we were ushered back upstairs to a small room overlooking Stonegate. They switched the lights out in this small room. We all stood quietly. "Can anyone tell me if they feel or sense anything" the ghost hunt leader asked. No-one said anything. Well "Here goes...", I thought to myself, clearly seeing a cot in the room from sometime around 150 years ago. "A baby died in her cot in this room," I said. The leader replied "Oh, that could be right, this room is known for the ghostly sound of a baby crying."

The baby crying is an example of residual energy. I had also seen and sensed a family around her, who were poor, and cold in the midst of winter.

We were then led upstairs to a large, panelled room with a huge round table that could seat approximately 20 people. Many of our party sat down, but I was one of the ten who had to stand. The event leader, a woman aged perhaps late fifties, came up to me and whispered, "What do you sense?" I told her that I could see clairvoyantly that this was a male meeting room. Women were not allowed in here, and women may still feel uncomfortable because there is a male watch-keeper in spirit telling any woman to get out. "That's right," our leader said. "This room was used for Masonic meetings." During our vigil in the room the guest clairvoyant tried to summon the spirits to do table tipping, but the table didn't move. The ghost hunting team picked up a voice on the EVP monitor saying: "Get out!", and the EMF meters kept flashing. Clairvoyantly I could see two simultaneous meetings of men being re-enacted. Both ghostly meetings were ignoring each other and ignoring us. The earliest dated meeting I could see was of men wearing wigs, possibly early 19th century, but I'm no historian. The meeting was emotionally charged because this group of men were mourning the loss of colleagues in some war, possibly fighting the French. There were empty seats, and the meeting was very sad and reflective, but being re-lived in spirit. The second meeting was of men sat in the same places, but from a later period, possibly late 19th century. They were all dressed in black suits and following very serious ritualistic procedures. Just why their meeting was still being re-enacted I couldn't get an answer to, but the emotions were dark, strict and of disciplinary fear.

We were then given a break. I went to the gents' toilet and spoke briefly to another attendee who said he had been on a few of these ghost hunts. "It must be exciting," I said. "Not really," he replied. "I haven't ever seen anything ghostly and it gets a bit boring." After the break we found ourselves being led further up narrow, uneven stairs to then be split up into smaller groups, each spending time in smaller rooms higher up. I was led with about eight others into a room where I immediately saw a very angry man, still grounded there in spirit. I asked him in my mind why he was angry. He told me that himself, his wife and children had all caught the plague and were forced to stay in the room. It was very hot, with no ventilation, and they had little food or water. The children had died first, then his wife, and then he had died. We were going back in time to the 17th or 18th century. I said nothing while the ghost hunt leader set up a table to try to get "The spirits" to do table tipping. I volunteered to put my fingers gently on the table, as did a few others. "If there are any spirits here then show us your presence!" exclaimed the leader. Nothing happened despite several repeated exclamations. I thought to myself that I had to say something. "Look, there is a man in spirit over in the corner who is very angry. Can I ask him to tip the table?" "Yes"... in an uncertain voice said the leader. So, I said, "Look, I can see you are angry, please move the table." The table started to immediately rotate strongly in a clockwise direction. The floor surface was uneven, but the table rotated firmly as though nothing could stop it. It didn't in any way seem frightening. "Ok, show us how really angry you are by making this table tip!" With that request the table lifted into the air and crashed sideways onto the floor. Others from nearby rooms came rushing-in due to the loud bang as the table hit the deck, and the lights were put back on.

We then were ushered upstairs into the attic. I was now suddenly surrounded by team members holding equipment near me as I gave an account of a cleaning lady who used to clean up this area, which had at one time been used as a grain store. However, in my vision I was then taken right back in time, prior to the house being built, prior to the monastery that had been on that site. There were big stones raining down on me, crushing those who had been on this site. Giant catapults were being used as huge weapons of battle to sling stones at those below in some battle. Was this from Viking times, or from Roman times? Again, I am no historian. This was simply residual energy capturing a very emotionally charged moment in history when many were injured and died.

I left the overnight vigil early, at 3pm. The final activity for the attendees was to conduct a seance, and I don't participate in seances. My reason is that during a seance we are inviting any spirit to make contact or do something. It can weaken our defence barriers to dark spirits, and I don't do that.

Hauntings that interfere with ordinary people living in modern homes.

I was called to a beautiful modern detached home. A normal respectable businessman and his wife had heard of me, and my ability to get rid of hauntings. Their three children, one young man, and two girls were in their early teens and very clued-up on being cool and fashionable. They seemed to view my visit with cool indifference. Their mum was certainly not cool. She was stressed and at the end of her wits. She immediately started to pour out an explanation of what was happening. Every night she would awake, pinned to her bed so tightly that she couldn't speak by some invisible force that she knew was an evil spirit. Her husband never witnessed this, but always slept through these incidents in a deep relaxed sleep. He had not experienced any weird experiences. She described lights flashing on and off and electrical appliances switching on and off, always when her husband was out. I spoke with the children who were not frightened but had heard footsteps on the stairs when no-one else was in the house, and all three had seen a ghost in the house, usually on the stairs. The ghost wasn't identifiable as male or female, but just a shadowy form.

Having listened to what they all had to say I firstly went to the stairway. There, hovering on the stairs was a grey mist. I knew this entity was the culprit, but what on earth was it? I then went down into the kitchen, directly beneath the stairs. I went alone. Confronting me was this grey mist, complete with a very scary head, menacing, and telling me to go. It was like a huge caterpillar, long, grey, hovering with this evil face in front of me. It was trying to scare me, but I was stronger. I knew this entity had been human at some time, but the person had been evil in life, and become so twisted in the afterlife as to completely lose its human identity. These things are depicted as fantasy in films that children watch. Our society is so misguided. These entities really exist and should not be taken lightly. I told the entity to go and leave this family alone. The entity became more frightening, came closer and gave a clear message that it was stopping where it was. For the first time I felt a shiver run up my spine. In the lounge I heard someone fall. A tough army friend of mine, a veteran of frontline fighting in Iraq, had been suddenly targeted by this spiritual energy, felt weird, very unwell, and collapsed. He had just come along out of genuine interest, but I feel also for his own amusement. He never expected this.

I had to think quickly and reverted back to my Christian Faith.

I spoke out loudly with a prayer to God. "In the name of Jesus Christ I command you to go." The entity retreated back. The solid walls of the house became transparent. I could still see this entity outside of the home, in the spiritual distance. "I pray to Father God to send the rescue Angels in to remove this entity." A beautiful Light appeared, and two Angels came out of the Light and grabbed the entity and took it away. My view of the scene became solid again, the walls of the house were now solid, and the entity gone. The atmosphere in the home had also, very suddenly, become normal, light, friendly, relaxed, and safe. I then asked my Angel Guide what had caused this evil entity to be in this house. I received a response immediately, now seeing clearly that the house was built on what is called a "Ley Line". These are lines of invisible energy criss-crossing the earth that were of great significance to ancient peoples because it is on these lines that Stonehenge, and other ancient monoliths were built. They are lines of intense spiritual energy. You know what? the ley line from their house also went straight through a hospital at the top of their road that at one time had been a sanatorium for people with mental illness. The time period of the sanatorium was around 100 years earlier. Quite a few lost souls were giving the residents of this new housing estate a scary time as I found out afterwards. I was subsequently called to clear several hauntings, both human and poltergeist, on this upmarket new housing estate. I feel sorry for others suffering such misery from evil spirits, or negative energy from misguided, lost souls. Many people suffer in silence, not knowing where to turn for help, and fearing that they will be ridiculed.

When I see children dressed like scary ghosts on Halloween, I don't find it child's play. I shudder and think "If only society, if only parents, knew the truth."

CHAPTER FIFTEEN

The Big Questions – The Bigger Picture

Questions that many people ask when contemplating the existence of a loving God

When children pass, where do they go? Do the Angels help?

What about the tragedy of women who suffer miscarriages during pregnancy? I cannot take away the pain that a miscarriage can leave with a mother and father. I have found that I can give a reasonably clear view of what happens to the spirit of the baby. I have given many people readings who have lost a baby in this way.

Children who pass: Do they stay the same age? Do they grow older in Heaven?

What happens to the soul of pets, such as cats and dogs who pass? In life many people observe that their pets, especially dogs, are very sensitive to the presence of angels around.

WHY IS LIFE SO HARD? HOW CAN THERE BE A LOVING, CARING GOD WHEN THERE IS SO MUCH SUFFERING IN THE WORLD?

"Heaven" is a place of love. Love is the air that we breathe. Why can't we just stop there forever?

The Centre of all consciousness is God or "The One" or "The God-Head". The One who gives us our purpose, is the Creator, and to whom we should always worship, praise and dedicate our lives in service.

Out of God is born fresh spiritual consciousness. New souls. This is a part of an eternal process of regeneration of the "God-Head".

New Souls are born with several basic needs:

A need to be loved

A need to Experience

A need to learn

New souls are given a duty: that is to GROW in love and care of each other.

If the souls in Heaven don't love and care for each other then Heaven itself couldn't survive.

New souls all have one basic "Fault". They (we) are in many ways self-centred.

A Comparison with real life

How does a good parent ensure that their child will grow to be a good, caring person?

Is the answer to protect the child, surround the child with love, spoil the child with everything he or she asks for?

Or is the answer to employ "Tough love"? Still loving the child, send him/her out into the world to experience and learn and grow as a person?

Well, God, our "Father" or equally "Mother" created the physical universe, created Earth, created life, and created our human bodies just for that purpose. So we could, as new souls, go out and learn the hard way to hopefully experience, through life, and learn and grow as people. The ultimate aim is to grow to be more loving and caring of others and be less self-centred. This enables Spiritual Advancement.

Many Lives

Of course in one life we may "get it wrong" or through tragedy or misfortune learn very little, and not advance.

However, through many lives we should all, except those who are evil, advance. Ultimately we will advance through many earthly lives, and then through Higher spiritual existence until eventually we converge and re-unite to become One with the "God-Head".

So, we are given lives which are meant to be both wonderful and hard, pleasurable and tough. Lives that are meant to experience every emotion from joy to despair, happiness to sorrow, good fortune and poverty.

Although this might sound odd, the harder the life we have, the more we are likely to learn and grow.

At the end of life's days all of us, except those who are truly evil, return to the sanctuary of love in the place of "True Reality", "Heaven".

"Heaven" is a very real place, and a place where we are given further instruction, and given lessons that help us learn from mistakes we made in life. We are shown the bad things we did, especially where we hurt others. We are also shown the good things we did, where we learnt to be more loving and caring.

CONSCIOUS ENERGY

I personally don't like the word "Spirit". It sounds a little creepy or un-nerving.

It is painful to think of a loved one, perhaps a mother or father whom we loved so much in life as now continuing to exist, but as a "Spirit".

We ask ourselves: "Have they changed? Has the person we loved suddenly become something different because they have passed to the other side of life?"

Modern society presents television, cinema films and computer video with the projection of "Spirits" as something to be feared, something unknown because we cannot physically see them, except for those who see a spirit appear as a ghost.

How can the personality of someone we loved so much whilst alive have changed so they now have to be described using the word "Spirit"?

THE ANSWER

As a clairvoyant I see all of us alive as a Conscious Energy. Conscious Energy is the "Me" or "I" inside all of us that thinks. We are all a thinking energy and we all possess AWARENESS.

When we are alive in our physical body we can be compared to the driver of a car. The real person inside is the driver. When we cease life in our physical body it can be compared to stepping out of the car. We shed the image of the car and appear as just ourselves. This I compare with what we describe as "Death". Yet we are still conscious, we are still aware, we can still think, and we are still the same person with our own unique character.

Clairvoyantly I see people who have passed to the other side of life as the same Conscious Energy. They are still the same person as they were in life. They have lost their physical bodies but can still feel they have a body. The other side of life is a familiar

place like going home. The memory of it is deliberately blanked-off before we are born so that we get the maximum experience out of physical life. Yet, because the other side of life feels more like home, more like true reality, and is full of love and where we belong, we realise that our physical life was the illusion.
So, when we die, we are still the same. We are still an energy of consciousness. I prefer to describe ourselves as that instead of "Spirit".

THE BIGGER PICTURE

The central point of all Conscious Energy in the universe is God, or can be described as "The God-Head" or "The Source" or "The One". The word "One" is important because we are all born out of one vast, incredible conscious energy. We are all still joined to this One energy. That is why it is common for people to think of themselves as the only "One" that is important. The most important lesson to learn from life is to become less self-centred and love others, knowing that they are all part of the same "Oneness" as ourselves.
Animals, and nature are also part of this "Oneness". Animals have smaller amounts of conscious energy, and nature has conscious energy flowing within. We must therefore love and respect animals and nature.
"Conscious Energy" is the only truth. Without Conscious Energy the universe would not exist.
So let us move forward in our thinking and understanding of what and who we really are... that is we all, each one of us, are right now "Conscious Energy" and you know what? that is exactly what we remain when we pass across to the other side of life.
I vote that we abandon the word "Spirit" to the religions, filmmakers and novelists of this world.

Who or what is God?
God is the centre of all Conscious Energy. Clairvoyantly I see that

in the Christian religion is revealed the true God, through Jesus' teachings. But what about the nature of God? Well, we are all born out of the Oneness of Conscious Energy that is called "God" or the "God-Head" or "The One". If we look at our personal driving force then we may have a clue as to the driving forces of God. Firstly, we all seem to have a need for constant EXPERIENCE. Work, study, relationships, sport, and hobbies are all fulfilling our need to survive, combined with our overwhelming need for EXPERIENCE. Even when we are sat, unless we are tired, we seek experiences of the mind through television, reading, computer games or the internet...or just social talk.

So, this would indicate that one of the driving forces of all Conscious Energy is the need to EXPERIENCE. God created the Earth, the physical universe, nature, and life so that we could have a place to live, to experience and hopefully to learn positive lessons that will help us spiritually progress.

Why Experience? Well, experience can be just for the reason of adventure or exploring. The prime reason though is to LEARN. So, another driving force of all Spirit is to constantly learn.

Why should religions teach that we should worship God? I agree that we absolutely must worship God on a daily basis. I spend my much of my life in worship of God in my thoughts. To worship in modern terms really means to show respect. Too many people think of themselves as high and mighty when there is only One High and Mighty. To worship God helps us realise who we are, helps in our communication through thought and prayer, and helps us to realise that we should thank God for the gift of life, and for all of the blessings in life. When things don't go right for us we should turn to God for guidance, healing and help in getting through our difficulties. Every good prayer is answered positively, although not necessarily with the answer we may expect.

God is of course LOVE. UNCONDITIONAL LOVE. The natural state in the "Spiritual Dimension" of Conscious Energy is that love is the air we breathe.

God is Eternal. Just think about this. This means that God has always existed and always will exist. We are children of God, born out of the Conscious Energy of God. So why are we still learning?

Why didn't we learn all our lessons at some point in the infinite past? Well this gives another clue as to the nature of God. It indicates that the energy of God constantly needs to renew. The renewal process is one where new spirit is born out of God. Spirit starts life as smaller life forms and gradually evolves into human life. As people our spirits grow through many physical lives. Eventually the individual spirits of people learn to become more loving and caring and wise to the extent that they no longer reincarnate into physical lives but continue their growth in the spirit world of conscious energy. Eventually this journey leads to mergence with the God-Head as a vast pool of intelligent, aware, Conscious Energy that controls the universe, and creates everything that is. The God-Head needs to continue to renew all over again by giving birth to new spirit. The journey of spirit then begins over and over again in a constant cycle of renewal.

Why Does the Energy of God Need To Constantly Renew?

Well, I hope you as the reader have been able to follow what are some very deep explanations concerning a subject that is perhaps too big a picture for many to understand.

The reason why the Conscious Energy of God needs to constantly renew is to keep love in Heaven totally pure, and of total integrity. Holy Scripture speaks of Satan being the "Fallen Angel". This is a primitive and simplistic explanation of what can happen in Heaven if Self-Centredness, the desire for power, and lack of consideration for the feelings of others gets a hold in Heaven. It would bring about destructive forces that would threaten the continued existence of Heaven with its atmosphere of absolute love, and absolute wisdom.

A Heaven of Eternal Love may bring about the restless qualities of Spirit that we see in life. For example, a permanent holiday in some kind of earthly paradise would still see some wanting more for themselves, such as personal power, and self-centred behaviour that would in some way cause suffering to others. It is a certainty that new spirit is born with a strong need for love, yet with natural self-centred behaviour.

I feel that the constant renewal of the vast Conscious Energy that controls the universe is a way that Conscious Energy relegates all the hard learning experiences to another dimension, the physical dimension of Earth and the physical universe. The physical dimension was created for this reason. So Conscious Energy, in the form of you and me, and all of life that ever was and will be, are together re-learning the hard way the need to be totally loving and caring of others.

THE SYSTEM WORKS. It is tough beyond tough, it is cruel in its most extreme forms at times, yet Love and Help from God through Spiritual Helpers, and from those loving , caring people who we come across in our lives on Earth continues to endure.

THE END RESULT IS THAT THE ABSOLUTE LOVE AND INTEGRITY OF GOD IS MAINTAINED FOR ETERNITY.

WHERE DOES ALL OF THE ENERGY OF THE UNIVERSE COME FROM?

The Universe in which we live is one huge dimension of unimaginable energy. Every star, every planet, every moon, all of life and everything we know is held together with invisible energy. Gravity demonstrates the unseen power of such energy. It's force keeps everything we know firmly on the ground. It keeps the Earth and Planets orbiting the sun, and the moons orbiting the planets.

Clairvoyantly I see that our physical universe is in balance with another very real universe - that of the so called "Spiritual Dimension". They are linked together through many a huge vortex. A manifestation of such a vortex is one found at the centre of every galaxy that remains a mystery to astronomers - Black Holes.

So, what is the truth about energy? Who put it there? How did it come to be?

Well, firstly the energies of both the Physical and Spiritual Universes are perfectly in balance. The energies are self-contained. Energy is put in place by God. "God" is the central point of consciousness, intelligence, and creativity.

If you imagine the energies of both universes are self-contained, then they cancel each other out. So, energy around us is in balance with energy in the spiritual dimension. Both are in balance, and like a set of weights on scales perfectly in balance, cancel each other out. Therefore, energy is self-cancelling. Energy negates itself through equal and opposite force. IT COULD BE SAID THAT ALL ENERGY IS AN ILLUSION. Think about this.. it is a profound, and very deep-thinking breakthrough in our understanding of the meaning of everything!

MANY DIMENSIONS

There are at least three dimensions identified in my research so far.

1) The Spiritual dimension of Heaven. I call this the "Dimension of Conscious Energy" This is the eternal place where "God" "The One" exists, out of whom we are born, and back to whom we eventually return.

2) The physical dimension. The physical universe of the Earth, Sun, Stars, Galaxies.

3) A dimension in between which is an intermediary place. This is necessary for the process of creation. Intelligent, Conscious Energy uses this place to move between dimensions in the process of creating and managing the physical universe and creating life.

OBSERVING THE UNIVERSE SPIRITUALLY LEADS TO A CONCLUSION THAT THE PHYSICAL UNIVERSE IS DELIBERATELY PLANNED AND

CREATED

Some examples:
The miracle of life. Darwin discovered that life evolved. So did the motor car. Each model of car basically has four wheels, a gearbox and an engine etc. The motor car has evolved over the past 100 years, yet each model has been deliberately designed and created, and retains the same basic structure.

So, if animals have similar basic designs in their skeletal structure how can we assume they haven't been created?

If a bird evolved, then how come that within one generation the bird egg also evolved? Impossible to see evolution working so fast or so cunning. Without the egg of course no more birds would have been born. Likewise all of life has seeds. A plant suddenly appearing would have to also invent its own seed in its short lifecycle or there would be no more plants of that kind.

Human beings suddenly appeared 4 million years ago. In one lifetime they, or their ape predecessors, would also have to invent the reproductive miracle of the egg, the womb, the sperm.

Let's now look at something so simple in the physical universe that it would take little thought to realise it could only happen by chance in billions to one odds.

The Earth revolves around the sun once a year, yet the orbit is within perhaps no more than a few thousand miles of what would either cook or freeze the planet. Secondly, the earth conveniently orbits so that the "Tilt" effect gives equal summer and winter to both the southern and northern hemispheres. If that didn't happen could life survive with one hemisphere in permanent winter, the other in summer? What would happen to our complex weather systems? Thirdly, the Earth revolves every 24 hours giving equal night and day around the globe. Fourthly, the moon has an important role to play in climate, tides and providing reflection of sunlight at night. Add together all these coincidences necessary to life and the odds against it happening by chance are perhaps in the realms of impossibility (this would be an excellent mathematical project!).

So, assuming (dare we?) that the Earth was deliberately, intelligently placed into orbit, what kind of immense forces are needed to achieve that?

If we can accept the theory of Creation, then which dimension existed first? Was it the physical dimension or the spiritual dimension of Conscious Energy? The answer again is simple. The only "Thinking/ Decision making" dimension is that of Conscious Energy. So, looking at this from a spiritual perspective, the conclusion is that spiritual dimension existed first. The Dimension of the Physical Universe was created by intent, by design, and with a most necessary purpose. The main purpose: to create a place where "Spirit", or as I call ourselves "Conscious Energy", can fulfil our overwhelming needs to Experience, to Learn, and to Grow in knowledge, love and understanding.

Looking at the vast scale of the physical universe, of creation of life, of the need to create an intermediary dimension, projects lasting so far many billions of years, then our inner need to experience reflects not only our nature, but the nature of "God", and opens the window to a fuller understanding of the meaning of life.

DO ANIMALS HAVE A SOUL?

The answer is YES! However, their conscious energy is not as big as ours. Imagine a large lake. An immense volume of water. Visualise this as being a sea of conscious energy. A tree, a plant, an insect might have one drop, like a raindrop of conscious energy. A dog might have a cupful of conscious energy. We as human beings will each have a bucket full of conscious energy. In other words our soul, the "I" or "Me" inside every one of us, is made up of conscious energy that is within all of life. Only we have more of it. Perhaps our inner soul is made up of the energies of many forms of life that have lived before. That is why in our imagination we can imagine being a tree, an insect, an animal. There is some part of us that lived lives in these forms at a time in the distant past. We can look at a dog and know there is someone looking back at us with less conscious energy as a soul, but still capable of feeling emotions of happiness and sadness, and still in need of love. Never forget though that all animals function by the pre-programmed instincts of their brain which take control of their behaviour when they are in survival mode. All conscious energy is born out of God, and still linked to God which gives us the individual feeling of "One" or "Oneness" with life. We all have soul mates and seek to find some of our soulmates as we journey through life. Ultimately, we may merge with our soulmates, after this life, or a future life, to become a larger oneness of conscious energy that moves as one through new realms of experience.

Everything that exists, that ever was, began in the Spiritual Dimension of Heaven. Heaven is headed by a vast conscious, intelligent energy that religions may call "God".
The qualities of the energies of Heaven are of ONENESS, and ETERNAL. There was no beginning and there will be no end. We will use the name "God" for ease of understanding
In the Spiritual Dimension there is no such thing as Time, but just the moment of "Now".
The Nature of God can be partly discovered by a logical examination of life on earth.
Firstly the "I" or "Me" inside each one of us is a feeling we have of Oneness. We feel this because we are all born out of this vast energy of God and are still linked to this energy whilst living in our physical bodies. The feeling of "One" often gives a person an "I" or "Me" sense of being of total importance and leads to self-centred behaviour. This self-centred behaviour can often lead to disregard and cruelty against other people because those who are self-centred find it almost impossible to understand that everyone is linked to the same oneness, with the same feelings inside. The human spirit in each one of us, born out of God, seems to show different levels of maturity in different people. Maturity is in this case being defined as degrees of capability in loving, caring about others, and realising that other people need love, help, and consideration. Also, that all of life is a part of this Oneness and needs to be looked at and treated with love and care.
If the Spiritual Dimension is Eternal, why does the human spirit

show signs of immaturity, a need to learn, and a need to grow? Why didn't everyone reach maturity somewhere in the distant past?

I believe that this question gives evidence that although God is eternal, the energy of God needs to constantly rejuvenate. New bundles of Conscious Energy (Spirits of people, of animals and life) are constantly being born out of God. They commence a journey through many lives. This journey is partly in the physical universe, such as in life on earth (and other planets), and also in the familiar true reality of home in the Spiritual dimension.

We discover another part of the nature of God by recognising our need for experience. Experience to be active either mentally in virtual worlds of television, computers, books, music, or physically in sport, work, art and craft, being creative, and in travel is a driving force in all of us. If we stand back and think about this need for experience, we realise that we are also glimpsing part of the driving force of God.

New-born conscious energy has one major fault, and that is self-centredness. Let loose in the Spiritual dimension, self-centred spirits would want control for themselves and threaten the continued existence of the Spiritual dimension of Heaven.

That is why the physical universe was created. Planet Earth is a learning ground where every experience is there. From the most extremes of cruelty and suffering, to the opposite extremes of incredible beauty and love, our lives on earth give us these experiences with one ultimate purpose: that we may eventually, through many lives, through many mistakes, through fortune and misfortune, learn to GROW in our love and care for others.

Our journey back towards re-uniting with the God-Head depends on how we progress in our genuine love and care for other souls. This is a strengthening, yet humbling journey towards taking our place in a more advanced role in the Spiritual dimension where we don't remain inactive. We learn that God's love for us is absolute, yet it is "Tough Love". We are not wrapped up in cotton wool but sent out into lives where often the experiences and learning curve are unbearably painful and difficult, yet equally they can be challenging and exciting.

There is also constant work in the true dimension of "Heaven". Such is the nature of God, and hence our individual spirits that our driving force even in spirit world is a need to continually evolve, and to continually learn and seek positive experiences.

The Afterlife is for the most part a world with a door that is firmly shut and bolted.
We are meant to live this life, fearing that this life is all there is. The reason? So that we get the most out of life and we don't try to get out of it when the going gets tough.
CLAIRVOYANTS and MEDIUMS have a gift that bucks the trend, that bucks the rules. They can see, in some way, through the closed door to the Afterlife.
The clairvoyant gift is meant to help people. In the afterlife there are intelligent, wise spiritual beings, including the Angels, and ultimately leading up to God. They can give a few people the gift of clairvoyance. However, they can also withdraw the gift if a clairvoyant becomes too successful at telling the world about what they see.
Clairvoyance is actually an energy. When I do readings I start off with a few minutes of very weak clairvoyant insight. Then, as the energy builds up what I see becomes clearer, and the readings become easy, rapid and accurate.

Helping people clairvoyantly is mainly intended to help people through life's most severe problems and suffering. Helping others on a one-to-one basis. If a clairvoyant misuses his or her gift, and especially if a famous clairvoyant is getting too good at convincing people with hard evidence of an afterlife, then the beings in the afterlife simply switch their clairvoyant energy off. This can make a fool of some famous clairvoyants who suddenly find themselves having to struggle to give readings to "Save face" when their clairvoyant gift has been deliberately cut off by those in Heaven. This seems cruel, unfair, but is necessary and intentional. The door to the truth of the afterlife has to be kept for the most part closed!

CHAPTER SIXTEEN

HEAVEN IS REAL

We have described that Heaven is Real in this book.

1) It is important to believe that we are spiritual and that there is an Afterlife. Heaven is our true, familiar home. Unconditional love is the natural state in Heaven

2) We have all lived through previous lives.

3) A Life Plan was determined for us before we were born.

4) WE each have a Guardian Angel to help us through life.

5) Our Guardian Angels knows our Life Plan.

6) Our memory of previous existense is deliberately blanked before birth.

7) Deep in our innermost being we still retain inner feelings concerning who we were in a past life.

8) We still retain inner feelings of our life goals in this life.

9) Our Guardian Angels accompany us throughout life and communicate through our INTUITION and FEELINGS.

We are constantly shaping our future

As a baby and infant we may still live in the spiritual state of living for the moment of "Now". We just see and react to the world immediately around us as.

As we get a little older we are then taught to think about the concept of "Future". A parent might say "You can't have that new toy today, but you can on your birthday". This educates our minds to start thinking about the future. Other examples "It's back to school next week" "You need to think about your future".

After that, the future is constantly in our minds. "I need to study and qualify for a career I wish to follow". "I want to meet the right person to have as a partner". I want to watch tv tonight". "I am watching my favourite sport at the week-end". "I am planning a holiday". "I am planning Christmas", and so it goes on. We cannot help thinking about the future.

Yet, we all fear the future. "Will I fail to achieve the qualifications that I need to follow my career choice?" "Will I suffer injury or fall ill?" "Will I ever meet the right person to share my life with?" "Will I have no money?"

If we make the decision to change our outlook on life, starting with the Life Statement we can focus on the future that we feel has been planned for us. No matter who we are this should in some way be a better, positive future. We may still have to face life challenges that we cannot avoid, so try to keep tunnel-vision focus on our life beyond that. If we see anything on our future plan that we might fear then make a prayer to the Highest in whom you believe to prevent that happening. As I have said earlier in this book I am no longer religious, yet I still pray to God. Coming from a Christian background I personally find that Christian prayers are extremely powerful and always receive a positive response.

I hope that this book has given you, the reader, an insight into how the future of ourselves individually, and for planet Earth can be seen. The book is intended to show that some of the meaning of life can now be revealed and explored. Heaven is Real. Nations could, if they wished, move forward from being technolgically advanced, yet quite primitive in spiritual knowledge, to becoming truly enlightened and able to perceive and change the future for the better in every respect.

CHAPTER SEVENTEEN

Clairvoyant Poetry

Grasmere Cumbria

Serene, beautiful, calm, majestic
Inspirational, classical, peaceful, poetic
All these feelings as I walked your path side
A mere not a lake, your calm water's wide
Deer Bolts Wood I roam, evening creeps up on me
Darkness comes quickly, I cared not, I was free
Of city life, suburban jungle, not really me.

Warm caress of summer evening, sky melted to a glow
Of fiery red between high mountains, natures beauty show
I wander now towards the village, warm hotel to be my host
Then I saw a light before me, my mind perplexed,
was this a ghost?
A light of white and strange in darkness, moving
yet there was no breeze,
Floating above, across the mere, meandering back into the trees,
Was this the soul of classical poet whose heart belonged to this
fine place?
Still dwells amongst this place of magic, where
early Springtime daffodils grace?

I felt no fear as light approached me, I was a stranger
in fairy land.

HEAVEN IS REAL

I had to know, I had to ask, who are you? my need to understand,
Then a whispering voice around me,
from the water and the land
"I am no ghost of classical poet, he was
my friend, he knew me well
I am an Angel, to care for nature, the woods,
the animals, 'tis here I dwell"

"This is a place of Angels, love and healing through eternity,
This evening, now, a special moment, all of life in harmony,
Remember this for all your years, know how precious life can be,
Please try to work to save our planet, for
poets of old, for you and me."

Derwentwater, Cumbria

Enchanted places on Earth
have many portals to Heaven,
Derwentwater, Cumbria is a place of them

I walked an easy path, through trees on Friar's Cragg
My spirit now uplifted, my weary feet didn't drag
Then, before my eyes unfolded the lake
and Borrowdale
Morning mist and distant mountains
rose-up to tell a tale,
Of majesty and wonder that many authors inspire
Poetic feelings intense, awakened, hearts that burnt on fire
To rest in this place forever, so many would desire

I spoke with my Guardian Angel, felt harmony inside
With all of life in nature
Joy I could not hide

A portal travels both ways, for those in Heaven
can still see,
This precious view that they experienced
when they were alive and free.

I see them with my clairvoyant gift
I hear the words that they once wrote
This place enchanted, I see more Angels
The moment forever caught
In my soul, my very being
That will live through eternity
I will return someday in spirit,
Heaven on Earth is where I'll be.

As I travel on Life's Journey, I have found that the best way of capturing my spiritual experiences is through poetry.

Is there a God?

My logic says I cannot see, a God taught by religions of all time,
So how can I explain my belief in God, in just a simple rhyme?
My clairvoyance is condemned by religions,
Yet through my clairvoyance I see
That there is a Source, a Oneness,
Existing throughout Eternity

We are all connected to the Oneness,
We are all children of the Love,
From the Source of all creation,
A vast intelligence from above

I see Heaven through my gift of clairvoyance,

For I am unconditional love,
I know that God truly forgives me,
My clairvoyance a gift from above.

Does Prayer Work?

In Heaven we still exist,
We are still the same, perfectly fine,
We can appear as we did in life,
Or as a soul, brilliant, Divine

We still experience, hear music, see,
The landscape around is so real,
Like a day on a perfect Spring Morning,
Flowers, vivid colours, and feel,
The air that we breathe as love
From the Source of all Purpose above.

We communicate in Heaven by thought
We just know how to do this, not taught
So, in our life on Earth learn to pray,
Anytime, anywhere, any day,
Pray to the Highest in whom you believe,
The One who loves you, makes you feel at ease
Who understands you, your good and your bad,
For the happy and sad times you had

You may pray to God, for healing,
For yourself, and those around who are feeling
A need for help in uncertain times,
The Guardian Angels with you,
Yes, BELIEVE, all will work out fine.

Having given over 6000 clairvoyant readings, the remarkable, unexpected aspect has been that many, many people have reported significant healing benefits from their reading. The obvious healing intention is to ease the pain of bereavement grief from those who received messages from loved ones who have passed. In addition to this people have reported genuine remission from cancer, more rapid healing from physical illness, rapid recovery from hip and knee replacement operations, and significant easing away of stress and depression.

When I give a reading, it is my Angel Guide that helps me by bringing me visions and messages. My Angel Guide connects with the Guardian Angels, who come in much closer when a reading is taking place, and of course Guardian Angels bring healing.

The following poem is a true account of a very real vision that I experienced that changed my life forever and gave me the strength and certainty to help people in a way that is hard to find elsewhere.

The Archangel

The first of May 1999, an Archangel appeared before me, Divine
Spring morning, sun shining, air sweet as wine,
Yet the beauty and radiance before me a sign...from Heaven

I bowed down in fear, but fear did not last
Archangel before me, from Holy Scriptures past,
His flowing robes, radiant, shone so bright as I saw,
A face of understanding, a moment beyond awe.
I was drawn to His eyes, full of love I was seeing,
He knew who I was, knew my life, knew my being
Unconditional love, and forgiveness for mistakes I was feeling

"Come with me" was the message, and I swiftly did rise
A path of light from Heaven, then to my surprise,
Into view came a place of landscape, beauty, so real
Green valleys, trees, flowers, vivid colours, I could feel

The air that I breathed was unconditional love,
All around me, surrounding, and a sense
of Higher Heavens above.

"This is "First Heaven", Archangel did say,
"A place of rest for souls when they leave life's day"
I could see people in joy, as they danced in this place,
Where all good souls enter from our human race
There were houses and gardens, and white buildings too
A library in Heaven holding a book of life for you.

Archangel, radiant, up again we did rise
To a Higher Heaven of cloud, and to my surprise,
Angels were working, planning and healing life
Helping those on Earth through adventures and strife.
The Angels nearby turned towards me and smiled,
They bowed down to Archangel, and I stopped for a while
Above me a Light of Third Heaven of our Creator
The Source of all Purpose, God of Love, and our Saviour
.....with the Father

"It is time to return," Archangel did say
"I have a purpose for you, to help others each day"
"The Angels will bring visions and messages to you,
For those in grief from bereavement, so
you can help them through"
"Another gift will be healing, though your body be weak,
The Angels will bring healing, for those
who seek...Healing from you"
"A gift of seeing the First Heaven, whenever you need
A gift of knowledge of Life's meaning
The Universe, the Seed...Of Life"

I suddenly was back, my feet on the ground,
Archangel was gone,
No-one near but the sound
Of a perfect Spring morning,

Birds singing around
...With the joy of Life
Robert Mason

Perhaps it would be good to stop in our busy life and feel the spiritual realities of beauty and peace...

In Stillness

In stillness, look at a beautiful flower,
A bloom of colour, and fragrance,
Nature's finest hour

In stillness, gaze at night-time sky,
The stars, the universe,
And wonder why.

In stillness, let spirit wander free,
Sense the love of God,
True reality.

In stillness, and peace,
Inwardly pray,
For strength and guidance
On life's difficult way.

In stillness you may find
That time matters not,
Timeless peace rediscovered
Perhaps almost forgot

Seeing The Future

What If...
The big things in our future are determined in our past,
Free Will just takes care of our everyday tasks.

We have no memory of past lives that made us whom we are,
Yet, deep-down feelings inside somehow seem to draw...

Our lives in a certain direction every time
Life can be good, can be hard, not always fine.

Our Guardian Angels know our Life Plan,
Whom we'll be, whom we'll meet,
The places we will live, every town, every street

If we live a bad life, our Guardian Angels won't be near,
We feel uncertain of the future, lives over-shadowed by fear,
If we stray from our Life Plan, make mistakes, go astray,
This is shown to us in Life Review, at the end of Life's Day

Try to be closer to our Guardian Angels,
We can do this by gaining empathy
for people, for nature... feel love and humility
Our Guardian Angel now with us, unconditional
love will set us free.

Intuitive visions of our future,
Two paths ahead will come to see,
We can change a path of pain
to a path of joy...true destiny

Mind thoughts are racing, if only we truly knew
This poem still holds a secret,
"What Ifs" can really be true.

INTUITION

Intuition emanates from our soul,
our inner being,
From within the realms and depths
of clear seeing.

Without eyes or words
A sense of just knowing,
the answers to problems

that have been growing.

Worries in our mind
decisions to make,
Crossroads in life
the direction to take.

Intuition comes quickly
when answers seem hard to find,
Sudden knowingness in seconds,
See clear, no longer blind.

Intuition stimulates our soul
to bring sudden wisdom,
To awaken mysterious whisperings,
once dormant within.

As wind rises from nowhere
where calm did prevail,
Whisperings in our mind begin,
lifting the veil,
To a connection with Heaven
and the Angels who help,
They can see a bigger picture
surrounding yourself.

Believe your intuition,
let inner wisdom guide,
Answers to life's problems,
will come from deep inside.

The Angels who've always loved you
will guide you from above,
They will show you what to do,
through their unconditional love.

A poem can sometimes help our understanding of the meaning of life

Our limited senses

Our physical senses are limited, and few,
There are many things we just accept
If but the truth we knew
We cannot see, touch, hear, smell or taste gravity
Yet, we can feel it,
Perhaps the strongest force in the universe
Science teaches, we believe it

We cannot see, touch, hear, smell or taste radio and
Television signals,
Around us, everywhere today,
carrying messages and entertainment they bring us.

We cannot see, touch, hear, smell or taste our soul,
Science denies our soul exists
Yet, our soul energy manifests in all
human expression, emotion,
and activity
This most important evidence science has missed

Oneness of Soul

Our soul energy is a conscious energy
It is all of whom we are within
Deep inside it is the "I" or "Me"
We may feel like the only "One"

We are all connected to a spiritual Oneness
In Heaven of the Spiritual dimension
Our true, familiar home,
Of conscious energy, love and creation.

Unity of Soul

If we cause hurt or harm to someone,
Or to any living thing that has a soul
We are really hurting a part of ourselves,
As some might say "Scoring an own goal...against ourselves.

Guardian Angels

Who or what are Guardian Angels?
They are people
Who have lived through many lives
Are spiritually grown, now sufficiently wise
To guide us through our lives

Their soul energy is pure and wonderful,
Radiant as the sun
Spiritual beings so beautiful
They bring the unconditional love of Heaven
They know our inner being,
Our mistakes, our good and bad, our feelings
Forgiveness isn't needed
For their compassion and understanding is absolute

The most important spiritual quality is to be caring to others, to animals and nature

A Person Who Cares

"Please find me food, I'm hungry,
Please give me water I'm dry,
Don't leave me, don't ignore me,
Or I will surely die"
"You are a stranger here amongst us
In this war-torn famine land
Please show me that you care,
Show me you understand"

The stranger stopped and said, "Your suffering I understand"
"I will lead you away from here,
Come, please take my hand,
To a place of food abundant
Where water freely flows
To a land of peace and freedom
Where children learn and grow"

The suffering all followed this stranger
Her goodness they all knew
Are you a caring person
Could this stranger, perhaps, be you?

Poems About Life

Just A Nrmber

To the world I'm just a number,
Along with all the rest,
Never getting anywhere or earning much,
Although I always keep trying my best
I know I'll never be famous,
And wealth never comes my way,
What little I earn goes on food and home,
As I struggle through each day.
So, what colour is there in my life?
I ask myself many times
The same work and routines every day
Are the usual experience of mine.
Yet what of the rich and famous
With their houses and property Fine?
For a person can only make use of
One room and one chair at a time
We are all breathing same air as each other
And, however our friendships are sought
The best and truest of friends
Can never, ever be bought.
A scenic view and the beauty of nature
Are things that we all can see,
And the experience of sport, art and music
Can cost little, and often found free.
So when I think of myself as a number,
It's only an emotional test
The truth is we all are important
Yes, you and I are as good as the Best!

Having done many thousands of clairvoyant readings, on every occasion the person in spirit comes across with their memories intact, and with the same character.

Memories

Days of old, days of gold,
My memories are as autumn shades
Life was "Nothing special" at the time
But looking back I can now define
Those special moments that stand out
With a warmth and fondness that removes all doubt
That the "Nothing special" was important to me
In this life that to others seems so ordinary.

The Spiritual Energies In Nature

The most important spiritual quality is to be loving and caring towards others, towards, animals, and nature and the environment. It is a measure of our spiritual growth.

Daffodil

Oh daffodil, your beauty of moment
Last forever, if time never spent.

All year you hide away from sight,
To appear in gardens as Springtime Light

Yellow radiance as the sun,
In coat of green your leaves are spun

Soft breeze caress, you move and dance
Flower of love, colour of romance

You are Spring, and Spring is you
You are my image of life renew

My spirit lifts with you nearby,
I scarce can turn away my eye

Oh daffodil, your beauty of moment
And eternal dreams forever dreamt.

Animals have a Soul

Little bird, enchanting song,
Perching in your tree,
Your tiny eyes look out,
Yes, you notice me.

My pet dog, he's so lovable,
I see happiness in his play,
He shows anger at a stranger,
sadness when I'm away.

How can my dog show emotions?
Animal is his nature,
Might the world believe all life has soul,
sometime in the future?

Religions teach animals have no soul,
Science says their brain inside,
Is nothing more than flesh and blood,
true spiritual nature denied.

I often feel that I can fly,
Or feel powerful like a lion,
I feel a part of nature
Yet, I'm a human being

I am clairvoyant and questions ask,
not to this world so wide,
I ask questions to the Angels,
answers come back from the other side
................of life.

Do birds and animals have a soul?
All life in nature too?
What is the human soul?
The response was surprising, new.

Our spirit comes in small drops,
like rain on ocean wide,
All living things have small drops,
of soul energy inside.

After many lives experience
in life of every form,
Small drops of spirit converge,
One larger soul reborn.

Souls of a thousand living things
come together just as one,
Emerging as a human soul,
a new oneness now begun.
Human soul is bigger than animal,
that cannot be denied,
Yes, when my dog looks in my eyes,
I know he has a soul inside.

The Pain Of Grief

My work is often to help ease the pain of grief when someone we love passes. We may never get over grief, but we can get through it, and move forward in our lives again...

Now you're Gone

You were here yesterday,
And now you're gone, passed away,
Cruel death has victory

News came swift that you had died,
It couldn't be, I screamed, denied,
Grief took hold, I cried and cried.

There are no answers from the world around
If you'd been religious would salvation
be found?

This busy world knows not what to say,
Like an express train on their way,
Material lives, living for today.

Science claims the answers in this modern world,
Life is dust to dust, so live to the full,
Young or old, boy or girl.

My grief takes hold and overwhelming,
Bewildered, lost, darkness closing in
Can't accept won't see you again.

My eyes are blind, but you can see,
I just don't feel you near to me.
Your soul is near, you still exist,
Life's cruel illusion is a mist

Your soul is free of all the pain,
Yet you're surprised, you are the same.
Heaven is beautiful, you know that now,
Others you loved are there somehow

Heaven is real, green valleys and trees,
Flowers caressed by gentle breeze,
Colours vivid, no pain, no fear,
A place like home made ready
for you there.

You try to reach to tell me this,
Yet the wall between us, impenetrable mist
of material world teaching,
Souls don't exist
Leaves me trapped in grief,
Time stops, I twist
...and cry.

Animals and Birds have a soul energy, not as big as a human soul, but still loved by God.

Little Bird

Little bird, on a tree branch up there,
Singing your song across the air,
A message to other birds, I am sure,
To me your song is pleasant and pure.
Little bird always seeking food to eat,
Then flying away to your safe retreat,
Little bird, you know how to make your nest,
Raise your young, and look your best
Little bird, little bird, on a tree branch, up there,
Singing your song across the air
You know love, you have a soul
I know you're aware...

Poems About Planet Earth

Life, where are you going?

Life, where are you going? as river, onward flowing,
Twisting left, meandering right, different
ways, new paths in sight
New things to do, feelings renew.

When the river flows calm and wide,
All seems well on life's journey ride,
River moves faster, playful dance,
Tumbling over rocks, scattered by chance,
Life moves faster, heart beats faster too,
We're high then low, happy, then blue.

Then, dance is echoed by thunder sound
Inside apprehension, roar all around,
River tumbles down rapid falls,
No more calm, rage crashing calls.
Life's storms will also come our way,
No matter sun or rainy day,
We're torn in half, emotional pain,
No calm, no harmony again?

Then, still and clear, fresh waters reach
In life new light, new hope, beseech.
Life, where are you going, full circle again?
Or some new twist in your hidden game?
As river meanders to distant sea,
Life's good times, and bad, steer my destiny,
With my love for nature, and our planet Earth
Guiding me.

The Beauty Of Our Precious Planet

Walking

A gentle Spring morning, the sun and blue sky,
delicate white clouds, floating high,
I walked up a steep path, into the trees,
Tall branches filtered sun, calm shelter from breeze.

A timeless rustling of leaves, restless movements of air,
As the wind high above rushed to who knows where,
Wild flowers of blue, lilac, yellow around,
Birds singing above me, their own sweet sound.

I felt at peace with the world, aware of creation,
A beautiful, warm, uplifting sensation.

I wandered endlessly on, not once did I tire,
'Till end of day came, the sky alive with fire,
The red, orange and purple, its beauty show,
Sunset o'er distant mountains, melted into a glow.

I prayed inwardly for our world, and felt heightened awareness,
My soul in harmony with creation,
Through nature's sweet caress

A "Calling"

Ever wondered why some people are so determined to do something to help others? Why some people are determined to work helping animals, nature, or the environment?

I believe that many people are given a "Calling". This is a gift from Heaven to do a particular task. The task is part of a Divine Plan to make sure that every aspect of life has people interested in caring and working to cherish, protect, repair and bring healing
Our Guardian Angels know this Divine Plan and work to help those with a Calling to help them fulfil their inner driving force to care for other people, or care for animals, nature, and planet Earth.

A Calling

Someone called my name, no-one there
I heard it again, from where?
Perhaps imagination, yet, inner-feelings, new sensation
Heightened awareness, inspiration.
I must help others, I must show care,
New ideas in my mind, guiding me – where?
Yes, I now see it clearly, people suffering out there.

I know it won't be a perfect way,
Somehow, I'll help others each day,
No longer thinking just about me,
Money, pleasure, living selfishly.

A new driving force, like fire within,
I must get started, I must begin,
Trying to help others, new goals in sight,
It matters more that I try,
Than to always get it right.

Touching lives, kindness, goodness, share,
Giving, helping,
My new purpose is to care.

Do we spend time earning money, polluting the planet, or do we focus our efforts on climate change prevention?

Money

When I think about money,
Food, clothing, home costs, are a problem sometimes,
And I need a little money for extra things
The interests and pleasures of mine.

I often wish I had money, my income a bigger share,
I could buy things I've always wanted, travel anywhere.

Yet, when I think of what I care for most, remind myself I try,
True friends, family, the beauty of nature,
Money just can't buy.

Conclusion

The Afterlife of Heaven is real and those in Heaven are working constantly through the many people who work in genuine love and care for others, for nature and for planet Earth.

There are over seven billion people alive on this planet and the future of all of us is as complex as each of the individual futures of the seven billion. I urge the world to believe that we are truly spiritual and that we can learn to recognise and act on the intuitive guidance that our Guardian Angels communicate. We can learn to perceive some of our future and change the future for the better. Together we can save planet Earth from the worst consequences of climate change. Individually we can in many ways learn to listen to Heaven so that we can stay safer, and work towards a happier and fulfilling future.

heavenisrealpublications@outlook.com

Printed in Great Britain
by Amazon